AN IRISH JAUNT
A Walking Tour from Dublin to Kerry

Cover: Tony Anderson on the road to Sneem, County Kerry; Macgillycuddy's Reeks in background.

'How are ye, lads?' – *on the road to Fermoy*

AN IRISH JAUNT

A Walking Tour
from Dublin to Kerry

Roger Jones and Tony Anderson

Illustrations by Edward Dowden

EX LIBRIS PRESS

First published in 1989 by
Ex Libris Press
1 The Shambles
Bradford on Avon
Wiltshire

Cover by 46 Design, Bradford on Avon
Typeset in 10 on 12 point Plantin by Saxon Printing Ltd., Derby
Printed in Great Britain by BPCC Wheatons Ltd, Exeter

ISBN 0 948578 13 0

For our fortnight's Irish jaunt we thank our wives, Hazel and Teresa

CONTENTS

Roger Jones lives in Wiltshire with his wife and three children where he has run a bookshop since 1980. Before that he worked in public libraries for ten years. He was educated at Gunnersbury Roman Catholic Grammar School (where he met Tony Anderson), Chiswick Polytechnic and The University of York. Between school and finally settling for the world of books, he worked at a variety of occupations, including washing-up, tin mining, metal-bashing (in Tony's father's factory), laboratory assistant, builder's mate and gardening. He wrote and published his first book (a town history) in 1979, since when he has been author of several more. He likes walking as a means of discovering places and meeting people. He also runs Ex Libris Press which publishes a number of books of (mainly) English West Country interest.

Tony Anderson lives in Surrey with his wife and three children. He was educated at Gunnersbury, then went on to Isleworth Polytechnic to do his 'A' levels, but left to take over his father's engineering business where he stayed until 1979. In that year he set up shop selling musical instruments opposite Hampton Court, where he found ample time to compose songs but not always such success in selling guitars and keyboards. The business closed down in 1983. Tony then gained a PSV licence and drove coaches for a short time. Eventually he began to work for a private employment agency where he is currently employed. His main interest is music and he has co-written and staged a number of musicals including *Noah, Scrooge, Bolonia* – based on the book *Peace in Nobody's Time* by George Borodin, *Water Babies, Alice in Wonderland, The People who walked in Darkness* and *Mary*.

According to Jones

Having enjoyed, in 1984, a long-distance walk from London, Britain's capital, to Land's End, its most south-westerly point, remote and staring oceanwards, it seemed an attractive idea to tackle a similar trek in Ireland, from Dublin to the tip of County Kerry. When my old friend Tony Anderson decided to join me, his father's home town of Dungarvan had to be included. Indeed, this became our half-way stage and an important psychological break in our journey.

I have long held that the best way to discover one's surroundings is on foot. The pace of walking surely lends itself to the appreciation of landscape and allows time to ruminate upon the people and places of the journey, and the real character of the country through which one passes.

The following account presents only one route through Ireland undertaken in too short a time. The great fascination of walking is its endlessness – the view around the next corner is always a bit different to the last, and often unexpectedly so. And walking encourages one to look back and to look inward as well as to look beyond.

Roger Jones
Bradford on Avon
Wiltshire
January 1989

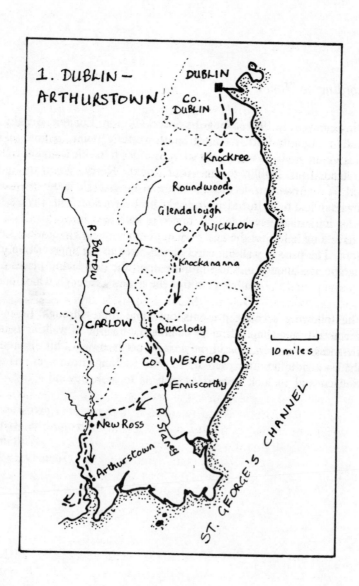

1. DUBLIN – ARTHURSTOWN

DUBLIN
Co. DUBLIN
Knockree
Roundwood
Glendalough
Co. WICKLOW
Knockananna
Co. CARLOW
R. BARROW
Bunclody
Co. WEXFORD
Enniscorthy
New Ross
R. Slaney
Arthurstown
ST. GEORGE'S CHANNEL
10 miles

Sunday 17 May

The room was around ten feet square and contained three bunk beds: accommodation for six sleepers. Paint cracked and flaked from the walls and pitched ceiling. All was lit by a single naked light bulb. This was not a cell in some neglected British prison but a male dormitory at Knockree Youth Hostel in the Wicklow Mountains, ten miles south of Dublin. It was May 17, 1987. Myself and a friend, Tony Anderson, had set out to walk from Dublin to the coast of Kerry in two weeks.

Our arrival at Knockree was later than I'd hoped although the day's light had not entirely drained from the sky as we reached our destination at around 10.30pm. Two of the lower bunks were already occupied and I let my companion take the third which meant I should spend the night some five feet above the bare concrete floor. It may have been the fear of toppling out that prevented me from sleeping until the Irish dawn began to illuminate the peeling paintwork and the face of my watch: it was 5am. Perhaps rather it was the jumble of thoughts and impressions that were racing through my mind. Twenty four hours ago I had been sleeping contentedly at home with my wife. Twelve hours back I had been sitting in a large and luxurious aircraft flying from London to Dublin. I had arrived at Heathrow well before the flight and had responded to a call to Mass in the Airport Chapel. Although I'd been baptised and schooled a Roman Catholic I had lapsed and after marriage was drawn towards Quakerism; this was my first Mass for at least 15 years.

I met Tony as planned at the *Aer Lingus* desk – he was in the clutches of a bad cold, looked pretty dreadful and had almost decided not to come. At Dublin Airport I had intended to purchase the necessary maps for plotting our route through Wicklow from the Tourist Information Office; this was Sunday and I found the office closed. I knew that the long-distance footpath known as the Wicklow Way began south of Dublin at a place called Marlay Park. After telephoning our wives from the airport to tell them that we had arrived safely (mine informed me there'd been an air crash that afternoon!) it was almost 5pm as we emerged.

I had planned to start our long walk by trekking along the first ten miles or so of the Wicklow Way from Marlay Park to Knockree. There was no time to ride buses so we approached a taxi driver. He was surprised to learn of our immediate and eventual destination ('I wouldn't drive to Kerry, never mind walking!'), indeed, he seemed unsure as to the whereabouts of Marlay Park and checked with some of his colleagues. When I asked how much it was likely to cost he replied straightway, '17 or 18 pounds'. I told him to step on it so that it might be less. This fellow in his beaten up Toyota took me at my word – we were touching 80mph on the dual carriageway from the airport and overtaking on the inside lane.

We raced through the city, which on this dull Sunday evening looked pretty unenticing. Those shops which were not empty or derelict were heavily defended with grilles and shutters, padlocks and alarms. It looked like a city besieged; I wondered how much worse Belfast could be in this respect. At the entrance gates to Marlay Park the taxi's clock indicated £14.80, so our driver, in his haste, had saved us a few pounds.

As we entered the park we saw the mountains close up ahead. Beneath the grey sky they seemed austere and rather threatening. In the foreground, beneath the benign gaze of a grand old house, the locals were gathering to leave the park after their Sunday afternoon stroll. There were crowds of children and parents pushing prams. We asked a buggy-pushing father the whereabouts of the Wicklow Way. He pointed us southwards along the path towards the dark swellings of the hills. We fortified ourselves with a swig of Irish whiskey from Tony's hip flask while I changed my trainers for walking boots.

The start of the Wicklow Way is indeed well signposted and we made our way along a tree-lined path adorned, at intervals, by some interesting pieces of sculpture. One was a group of three enormous upraised hands, palms outward, not the forbidding Red Hand of Ulster, but the hands of gentle giants carved in wood. Another was a standing female nude and yet another a miniature submarine, black and rather featureless, half-submerged in a pond, – this would have been sinister had it not been so toy-like. After the park the Way began to ascend, first along a lane flanked with hedgerows highlighted with the white stars of stitchwort, then by a track through Kilmashogue Forest where the views across Dublin grew wider and more extensive with our every step.

We approached a man strolling ahead and asked how long it would take us to reach Knockree Youth Hostel by the Wicklow Way. This fellow had a splendidly clear way of talking and told us that we would reach a valley where conditions underfoot would deteriorate; we would then need to scale another mountain before descending to Knockree. This was the one occasion when such an enquiry elicited an informed and reliable answer. We soon learned that most people, rather than disappoint the enquirer by admitting ignorance, would invent something just to please. We realised that it was a good few miles and he was not completely reassuring about our reaching the hostel before nightfall. I was keen to get there; in fact, we had no choice, except perhaps to head coastwards to Enniskerry. Now we'd stopped I glanced at Tony and was shocked to see his face - it was puce, an abnormal colour indeed.

Three Rock Mountain – Sugar Loaf in the right distance

Some time after this encounter the helpful yellow arrows denoting the course of the official footpath dried up completely .... it was somewhere beneath the summit of Kilmashogue Mountain that we became unsure and lost our way. We reached a high point at Three Rock Mountain, crowned with a TV mast, and took in the view, from an altitude of around 1500 feet, towards Bray, the sea and the mountains further south. Soon after this we completely left the Way and I resorted to following my nose - a highly doubtful method of navigation.

In the *An Oige* (Irish Youth Hostels) Handbook is a jolly colour

11

photograph of young people walking near Knockree Youth Hostel. In the background is the distinctively conical, almost volcanic, outline of a mountain silhouetted against the sea. I could see this same mountain as we stumbled and splashed down through a bog to reach a lane. If we kept that mountain in our sights and headed to its right hand side I reckoned we would be moving in the right direction.

Tony asked directions at a roadside cottage. A lady told us to carry on and turn right at the crossroads ahead. Here was a pub and by this time we both felt in need of a drink and a bit of reassurance. Irish pubs are often not obvious - their function betrayed only by one small sign bearing the Guinness logo. We walked around and eventually found an unlocked door leading to a huge lounge bar, somewhat austere, but a place for a serious evening's fun.

We asked for two pints of Guinness for which we were charged the large sum of £1.46 per pint; upon enquiry we were told that this included the cost of entertainment – a band was tuning up on the far side of the room. We got chatting to the barman, a good looking young chap who knew nothing of the Wicklow Way – he was a stranger in these parts, from Kildare, all of 25 miles away, 'Have you never been to Kildare?', he wanted to know, then told us of his intention to learn the barman's trade and to move on to a Union bar in Dublin; as he spoke to us he demolished several beermats by methodically picking them to bits. It seemed an odd ambition – he explained that his father had a small, 100 acre farm and three sons. There was not room for all of them and this cheery fellow would aim to be a 40 hours per week (plus paid overtime) Union barman in Dublin.

We decided to move to the smaller bar at the front of the pub where the Guinness was cheaper and we were shielded from the raucous tuning up noises of the band for which we had to pay extra. We ordered some cheese sandwiches and as we ate them the bar rapidly filled up. A mother came in and bought a Chomp Bar for each of her three scraps of children.

Thus fortified and cheered we walked several more miles in the twilight and eventually arrived at Knockree Youth Hostel. Staying there was a large party of teenage girls, some of whom offered us a seat in front of a sweet-smelling turf fire and from whom we scrounged milk for a cup of tea (I'd packed a few teabags). We shared a room with two English university students. No food was available at the hostel and our breakfast consisted of tea and the remains of the pub's cheese sandwiches.

Monday 18 May
Tony was completely new to walking and youth hostelling and, on an empty stomach and nursing a cold, was perhaps not greatly relishing the first day's walk. My own spirits rose as we set out from Knockree. The view across the Dargle River towards that volcano-like mountain – in fact known as the Great Sugar Loaf and more impressive than its 1,654 feet would suggest – was an inspiring start to the day's adventure. We entered a forest and followed the signposted Way to a rustic wooden bridge across the Glencree River; on the far bank the path became indistinct and it was a real struggle through the undergrowth and across the boggy ground. This was followed by a scramble up a steep slope to reach a forest track. Tony was slowing down and pausing for breath. I was trying to encourage him but beginning to feel worried and very guilty about dragging him across Ireland with me.

At this time the day before he had probably been enjoying a leisurely Sunday morning breakfast. The walk across Ireland was still in the mind; it would be an adventure, a bit of fun, something to tell the grandchildren. Now it was a slog on sore feet and aching legs, along hard tracks and across soft bogs, staying in youth hostels cold and austere. Tony Anderson, my soul-mate since we became friends at school over a quarter of a century before was also Tony Anderson, high-powered executive, recruiter for computer salesmen, Volvo driver, former Labour councillor now Baptist church deacon, song-writer and musician, three quarters Irish but life-long resident of Surrey, a happily married man with three sons, two of them bigger than himself. Yet here he was, bending under a rucksack, twice as heavy as mine and from which an enamel mug dangled, plodding across some God-forsaken Irish hillside, thinking dark thoughts or most likely thinking of home. But in truth, in many ways he'd had a hard life, and old Tone was not one to complain. In contrast, I was actually enjoying the prospect and relishing the first full day's tramp. I felt alternately elated with myself and deeply concerned for my friend – I wanted him to be elated too but knew he couldn't be, not now.

We struck along what seemed an endless track through a dense and gloomy pine plantation, a monotonous prospect relieved by the occasional glimpse of deer and the summit of the Sugar Loaf in the distance. We emerged from the forest to be confronted by a great natural amphitheatre with Powerscourt Waterfall as its central feature. The steeply sloping sides are bosky and rugged, an ideal habitat for ravens, several of which we saw wheeling about. We rested before following the path above the slope. The Way becomes obscure and we descended to the river as it begins to plunge down the silvery schistose rocks, where deep pools reveal the water to be brown and peaty yet clear. We drank both from the Dargle River – a gargle of Dargle – and from Tony's hip flask. Neat whiskey is perhaps not the best remedy for a flagging frame and an empty stomach.

We'd lost the path again. My half-inch to the mile map was too small-scale to gain any but the most general impression of the route to be taken. We picked our way upstream but did not find the expected bridge. Instead we stepped across boulders to reach the opposite bank. Here was a wide green road – flanked by the forest to the left and a stone wall to the right. Beyond the wall lay the hinterland of the Wicklow Mountains – a barren, treeless landscape of gentle, sweeping slopes. The Wicklows are granite mountains, the rocks at Powerscourt Waterfall represent the metamorphic contact zone between the intrusive, igneous granite and the surrounding country rock, thus marking, in a dramatic way, the boundary between the two.

Our road was uphill; Tony was becoming slower and slower. I went on ahead to encourage him – perhaps this discouraged him. The path followed the forest boundary to the left. The Wicklow Way on the eastern flank of Djouce Mountain lay ahead; Tony was out of sight and I waited. I eventually saw his head bobbing heavily, stopping every minute or two. He drew up and I could see he was all in. He'd drunk more whiskey, his heart was racing, he felt weak and faint. I tried to jolly him up but after a few more paces he dropped to the ground, lying flat on his back with his arms outspread, like a man crucified. He had evidently passed out, his breathing was laboured and irregular. I sat beside him praying that he would at least continue to draw breath and trying desperately to remember how to administer artificial respiration. After a while his breathing evened out and he seemed to be enjoying a deep sleep.

When Tony awoke he said he felt rather better. Thank God! I carried both our rucksacks and we continued, not by the Wicklow Way to Djouce Mountain but beside the forest until we reached the road. Tony was now much more talkative and made good progress. I regretted forsaking the official route but at least Tony had cheered up and I felt that we could reach our target for the day: Glendalough. Now we followed a road for many miles south crossing several streams which drained the mountains to the west to fill the reservoirs to the east. It was mid-afternoon when we reached the village of Roundwood. The pubs and restaurants were shut but we found a shop, bought a basketful of groceries and sat down on a bench to gorge ourselves: bread, cheese, tomatoes, yogurt, apples – this uncooked feast gave us the strength to carry on.

I felt relieved at Tony's regained sense of humour but still worried that perhaps this was all a bad idea and that he should give up now and go back home. We agreed that he should make his own way from Roundwood to Glendalough by the main road. He could hitch a lift and I would meet him at the hostel. I wanted him to find a space in which he could assess the situation, without me around, and decide whether he wanted to carry on or give up. Meanwhile I headed west from Roundwood and regained the Wicklow Way – actually following a lane below Lough Dan, then past Glendalough House. Here I saw some very efficient looking farmland – stone walls in excellent repair, fields clear of rocks and thistles with good thick grass on which grazed fine red cattle and sheep freshly shorn. This was a productive valley but supported only cattle and sheep: there was no grain or potato growing or market gardening. I eventually spotted a yellow arrow at the roadside and followed the Way uphill along the edge of a forest. This took me up to the summit of Paddock Hill, well over 1,000 feet, from which I had a great view over the valley to the mountains.

I arrived at Glendalough Youth Hostel to find Tony already there, looking and sounding happy and confident. We checked in, though in the absence of the warden (at 7pm a note on his door bore the message 'Back Soon' – he turned up an 11 o'clock). We shuffled up-valley, past a tiny ruined church to the Royal Hotel where we were too late for food. Great! We walked back a mile to the Heather Glen Restaurant which the grocer at Roundwood had recommended. As the only customers we were given an excellent meal of monumental proportions. Tony's Irish stew was a potful sufficient to feed a family of four; my trout was not one but two large and sturdy specimens served with two sorts of potato and four different vegetables. We could not finish it all but immensely enjoyed what we could manage. That night we slept the sleep of the physically exhausted and well-fed. Things were beginning to look up; I felt I had finally arrived in Ireland and that the next day must be a great one.

Before I fell asleep my mind drifted back to the time of my first visit to Ireland, in 1970, a few months after I got married, and to an old Irish friend, Tom Dingle ....

My wife had a predilection for western and northern climes whilst mine was for sunny southern ones. Her grandmother had been a McAuliffe from County Cork. In fact her great great grandfather had come to England during the Famine, so no doubt she had a natural affinity with the country. We began our 1970 holiday in Belfast where we stayed the weekend with a young couple – Hazel had met Gavin youth hostelling. His new wife was not over-friendly – they were Protestants and possibly disapproved of our 'mixed marriage'. After Belfast we hitchhiked along the Antrim coast and eventually reached Derry where, spat at and made to feel decidedly unwelcome, we rode a bus across the border and stopped a couple of days in Buncrana, County Donegal. Here we found a bed and breakfast where we were asked by the landlady most pointedly whether or not we were married, evoking a kind of indignant embarrassment. I remember the bedroom contained a collection of holy statues which all seemed to be staring at us. When it was time for bed we felt a strong urge to undress with the light out. We greatly enjoyed Buncrana – the singing bars and relaxed atmosphere; if Buncrana was typical of the Republic then we felt this was a different country to the one we'd left behind in the Six Counties.

When I left university in 1969 (the year before we visited Ireland) I returned to my vacation job as a gardening labourer for the local council. One of my great friends there was a middle-aged Irishman by the name of Tom Dingle, from Castlebar, County Mayo. He was a tiny fellow with a large hairless cranium and a pair of thick lensed glasses, a great prankster and story-teller. We certainly did not kill ourselves working. Much of our time was spent in huts sited in various parks and open spaces, drinking tea, smoking roll-ups and setting booby traps for the keen young foreman. Old Tom had been a gravedigger in Ireland and had some spooky tales. He'd never had a son and we found an immediate rapport. One morning he found his Irish wife dead in bed. After this he hit the booze in a big way though he was perhaps saved from drinking himself into an early grave by marrying the barmaid from his local. I acted as best man at their registry office wedding. Soon after that I left London and we lost touch.

In the meantime, during our holiday in 1970, we visited Tom's daughter in Castlebar where her husband was caretaker of the local pig processing factory. We were cordially invited into their home and plied with lager and large whiskies, then taken on a guided tour of the works and led into enormous cold rooms which held an endless array of pig carcases. Later we were offered sausages and rashers but had to decline after the experience of facing so many raw, dismembered pigs.

Our week's touring was followed by a week in a caravan in Connemara. Our site was on the Hill of Doon which projects into Lough Corrib – the hillside faces due west – about three miles from the nearest village. The weather was pretty lively, with a strong wind blowing along the lake and up the slope. On the far side of the water were bare black mountains and, between them, a great featureless bog, now shrouded in mist, now visible as far as the eye could see. Such wild and desolate landscape, together with such unpredictable weather, was completely new to me and I found it scary. That night the wind blew fiercely and we spent a sleepless time, jumping out of the caravan more than once when we felt it being lifted off the ground. We left the next day but stayed in Ireland, bed and breakfasting and youth hostelling, until our money ran out, when we returned to England from Dun Laoghaire.

Tuesday 19 May
Tourists flock to Glendalough to visit the myriad remains of the ancient Christian settlement and to marvel at the natural wonders of mountain, valley, lake and forest. We had no time for such aesthetic pleasures. Having but two weeks to reach the Atlantic on foot, we had to content ourselves with an inspection of one ruined church and a glimpse of the mountains to the west. We set off, for the fourth time traversing the same stretch of road, past the Heather Glen Restaurant to Laragh. Here Tony posted some of his extensive wardrobe to his aunt in County Waterford, where we intended to be by the weekend.

From Laragh we began to ascend the Military Road, a well built highway constructed by the British following the 1798 Rebellion, in order to allow rapid movement of the occupying troops to trouble spots. After a mile or so climbing the Military Road the Wicklow Way leaves the road and heads off in the wrong direction altogether to take in the 2,000 feet plus Mullacor Mountain and the forested slopes above Glenmalure. This seemed an unnecessary detour and we continued along the undulating road. The motor traffic is very light and does nothing to detract from the pleasure of walking through this gently mountainous landscape. Yet these mountains are largely barren, forestry being about the only use to which they are put. The sheep and stone walls to which one is accustomed in the English Peak and Lake Districts are here entirely absent. There seem few signs of human settlement – either present-day or in the past. In fact County Wicklow, owing to its dominating mountains, has never been Ireland's most prosperous region though, like the rest of the country, it did once support a much larger population.

The immediate view from the road out of Laragh was marred by quantities of garbage. Wherever there was a handy shoot from the roadside, often over a bridge into a stream or simply into the edge of the forest, people had dumped old cars, household appliances of all

Abandoned car – a familiar crop

sorts, piles of old bottles, anything and everything. The countryside was not The Countryside – if it was not used for agriculture or building it seemed to constitute in the minds of many simply waste land, to be used as such. When I had been a garden labourer, one of my jobs with old Tom Dingle had been to muck out the rose beds on council estates. Having completed the job we would usually have a fag break. If it was Tom's last cigarette he would invariably toss his empty packet into the freshly raked flower bed and saw no contradiction in this.

We met a fellow clearing a ditch at the roadside. He was a stocky figure with a moon-shaped face, a bright red complexion, startlingly blue eyes and jet black hair. He'd lived in England for many years but, following an illness, had come home to convalesce, got married and not gone back. He admitted that jobs and good money were to be had in London but he did not seem to regret that he was now missing out on them. We had seen many notices declaring 'Poison Land' and enquired of him what this referred to. He told us that poison was laid to deter dogs and foxes though he would not consider doing this himself for fear that children might get hold of it.

Five miles on the Military Road through forest and bog brought us to a crossroads at the foot of a steep, narrow valley which pierces the high mountains like a knife. Four miles to the north-west, at the valley's head, is Glenmalure Youth Hostel. Immediately at hand was a hotel where we stopped for a drink. Tony ordered lemonade with lime which turned out to be brown like the peaty bog water. Lemonade in Ireland is white or brown, in this case the lime had been added to the latter variety. The barmaid and handful of customers were not unfriendly but we did not fall into conversation.

The interior of the bar was sombre. Plain walls of a dark hue featured two framed items – both were newspaper cuttings describing former battles fought hereabouts in which the Irish were victorious. One occurred in 1580 over the Elizabethan settlement and one in 1792 – the Desmond Rebellion. Our surroundings are significant – the colours, shapes and appearance of the everyday world in which we move affects us deeply. In Ireland one is aware of a general drabness and frequent conflict of images. Dervla Murphy in her book *A Place Apart* (Penguin, 1979) poses a pointed question when she asks: 'How is it that the race bred in this lovely country has never developed a sense of visual beauty?'

From 400 feet at Glenmalure we passed the empty shell of the former Drumgoff Barracks and climbed up to 1,500 feet – here we looked back for the last time at the distinctive Sugar Loaf Mountain – some two or three miles through forest and gradually descended to Aghavannagh. Lugnaquillia, Wicklow's highest mountain at over 3,000 feet and with its head in the clouds, was our constant companion along this stretch. The hinterland hereabouts is used as a training ground by the Irish Army and notices warn of the proximity of a firing range, another of unexploded bombs.

In fact, the silence around here was almost audible; it was a living presence, rather than the absence of life and movement. The day was overcast though rainless and there was hardly a puff of wind. On occasion one was fooled into thinking a car or train was approaching

Glenmalure: Ruins of Drumgoff Barracks built, with the Military Road, after the 1798 Rebellion. The original Barracks were destroyed but later rebuilt.

when in fact it was only the breath of a breeze in the tree tops. It seemed the whole country was soundly asleep. Just then a little old lady came towards us; she was surprised to hear we'd walked from Laragh but assured us,

'Hiking is good for you. You'll sleep well'.

She departed with a blessing, 'God be with you'.

From Aghavannagh we climbed up to over 1,000 feet for the third time and began to leave the mountains behind as we gradually descended through a sparsely populated stretch of country to reach the spacious and rather modern looking village of Knockananna. It was early evening as we entered the pub. We ordered a pint and asked about accomodation. We were told there was no place to stay in the village and that we would have to go on to Tinahely, several miles away. We were convinced there'd be somewhere to stay here. The lad serving behind the bar eventually went off and returned with the landlady. She was a woman in early middle age, large and confident, capable, motherly, reassuring. She would surely get us fixed up. She sent out a smaller boy on his bike to ask someone down the road who had not a telephone whether he could take two men. He came back and said we'd be OK.

Our pub landlady cooked us a meal of sausages, rashers, eggs, chips and salad (including red pepper), pot of tea and bread and butter. As a half-hearted vegetarian, these were the first morsels of dead pig which had found their way past my lips in almost a year. They were not to be the last. Sausages and rashers are apparently Ireland's staple diet and to Bed and Breakfast in Ireland is to start each day with a large chunk of pig.

As we ate our fill we got chatting to an old man at the bar. He was drinking Guinness and shorts – he managed to find the money to afford Ireland's high bar prices while his wreck of an overcoat was fastened with safety pins. Our companion told us about past battles in the area, without rancour for the British, but with a sense that these hostilities, enacted some centuries before, had occurred during the past few years. As I set off for our digs he assured me that it was 'not half a mile' – but omitting to say whether it was more or less.

I set out, on the road north. It was now a glorious evening. The sky had cleared completely and in place of lowering cloud, the sky was an unbroken blue and the air brighter than it had been all day. After 20 miles with a good meal and a drink or two under one's belt, a fine evening and the prospect of a comfortable bed, I fairly skipped along the road. I found the house: a modern bungalow on a large plot of land which itself would cost a fortune in southern England.

A youngish fellow answered the door and I entered, explaining that my friend would soon be following, that he was telephoning his wife from the village and that I had already rung mine. I welcomed this opportunity of informing him that we both had wives, that we weren't a couple of gays from England. I soon learned that this was an unfounded anxiety; the single state is commonplace in Ireland. The Irish are very relaxed about all sorts and conditions of people and don't possess many of the preconceptions and hang-ups of the English. The fact that we were two greying Englishmen carrying rucksacks across Ireland did not seem to put people on their guard at all. At least this is the impression I got. I have since spoken to a friend of Irish parents who assures me that there is no snob like an Irish snob and that proof of this is that great store is set by finding a marriage partner from a suitable background, and this can be very narrowly defined. Certainly my reading of Irish fiction seems to bear this out, but I can only comment from my experience and I would testify to the friendliness and openness of the Irish people.

The man of the house showed me our room and apologised for the double bed – a small one at that. My bath was indescribably enjoyable. Our host's name was Eddie and his children were Christine, Edward and Gary, respectively about ten, eight and six years old. The daughter was a delightful child, already possessing that confident and reassuring manner peculiar to Irish women. After our ablutions we were hovering in the hallway when she asked us into the back living room. Dad smoked and offered us cigarettes; we declined. His offer of bread and butter and a pot of tea we accepted and enjoyed his home-made soda bread. Christine was learning to play the guitar. This instrument promptly found its way into Tony's capable hands and pretty soon we were enjoying a sing-song, or 'crack', by going through Christine's song book, which included *The Wild Rover* and such like. The two brothers got out of bed and joined us. Making music had melted every trace of ice and left us all firm friends.

Wednesday 20 May
Breakfast was more than ample and we shared our table with two scruffy young men who were working for a spell locally. When Tony told them we were walking to Kerry, one exclaimed, without apology, 'F**k that!' As we set out the family came to shake hands and wave us goodbye. Eddie's wife was home from the night shift in a distant factory, while Eddie – a trained chef but out of work, 'I don't do anything, to be honest with you' - acted as househusband. He burnt turf which he cut himself; a winter's supply costs him around £70, payable to the farmer for his plot. Its disadvantage is that it leaves a lot of ash and the chimney has to be cleared once a month. And of course it has to be cut though the traditional slane (turf-cutting spade) has been replaced by a machine.

Eddie seemed quite emotional as we said goodbye. The morning was as glorious as the previous evening and we set out, at first back to the village, with happy feelings. Our bungalow was the furthest from the village – the setting was idyllic. Mountains not close and forbidding, but swelling and dipping along the horizon, like a line of exquisite music, the foreground a gorse-studded expanse of fields and bogs. It seemed you could walk uninterrupted in any direction, the view was panoramic.

Our host's car overtook us as we approached Knockananna and we waved to his children as they hopped into school. We set out on the road south hoping to reach Bunclody in County Wexford by the evening. We certainly had a long walk ahead of us. It was a perfect day and now the country was greener, more productive. There were plenty of forested hills over a thousand feet but they were the mere remnants of the Wicklow Mountains and separated from one another by well farmed valleys. A trailer-load of wool passed us, then we saw some haymaking in a field. I began to relish these evidences of agriculture, a reversal of one's usual feelings in the over-populated, over-exploited landscape of southern England. There one yearns for a bit of wilderness, land as nature intended it. Now, after three days of the wild Wicklow Mountians I was enjoying the prospect of efficient farming, like some gentleman traveller in the Georgian Age, looking for signs of improvement in the land.

At Bridgeland crossroads we were unsure of the way. My preference was to avoid main roads and stick to lanes wherever possible. The latter obviously carry less traffic but are also often more direct routes. On this occasion, following my nose led us along the right way. Very soon there was a church and then a shop. At the latter we asked for a large bottle of lemonade.

'Do you want it wrapped?' asked the shopkeeper.

'No, we want to drink it now', I replied.

'Sure, that's the best way of carrying it', says he.

We carried on until we reached the main road which ran along the valley to Shillelagh. Here I failed to find an alternative minor route. At the junction there is a large Celtic cross commemorating the men who fell in 1798 against the British. This was one of many reminders of Ireland's protracted struggle for independence. This long history must affect the Irish conscience in a way which is very hard for the English, who have not been invaded or occupied since 1066, to appreciate. In this respect Ireland has more in common with the ex-colonial nations of the developing world.

On the road to Shillelagh was a notice indicating a 'Water Supply Scheme for Tinahely, Carnew and Shillelagh – financed by the EEC'; in Shillelagh itself a Youth Centre was being similarly provided. Joining the Common Market has evidently had its advantages for Ireland, not only in the form of farming subsidies.

In Shillelagh we stopped at the Avalon Hotel for a pot of tea and a sandwich and, refreshed, crossed the bridge over the Shillelagh River to tramp a long, often straight and therefore occasionally tedious, road to follow the valley to Clonegal. Somewhere along this road we passed from Wicklow to County Wexford. At Clonegal we were very tired and lay down on the roadside. I crossed the bridge to reach a shop for ice lollies and drinks. In doing so I set foot in County Carlow. We summoned all our strength to cover the remaining few miles to Bunclody. Unfortunately we missed the short route which climbs a small hill to Bunclody directly but took a road which describes a great loop to the west, following a meander of the river, now the Slaney.

It was around 8 pm when we reached Bunclody; we felt we could not have walked another yard, but were forced to in search of digs. People were flocking into the town in anticipation of the Hang Gliding Championships which were due to take place at Mount Leinster at the weekend. We were eventually directed to a Mrs Deane who ran a large guest house in the main street. We were given a double room, prettily decorated and furnished with some good solid pieces in dark polished wood. After a clean up we shuffled out in search of food and drink, not in that order. We found a high street bar for our first pint of Guinness. Inside were one or two drinkers and an academic-looking, middle-aged man serving; I guessed he was the owner. The bar was small and comforting, rather than comfortable; an enormous clock hung on the wall, ticking reassuringly.

Our two glasses of stout were filled at the hands of an expert, one who is utterly sure of his craft. First half a pint was allowed to settle, then it was added to, and added to again. The fascination of watching Guinness being poured never weakens. The dense, dark liquid, as black and impenetrable as tar, provides a striking contrast to the creamy smooth head. Equally compulsive is the extraordinary phe-nomenon of what appear to be bubbles descending against the side of the glass from the head to the liquid below. These are not actually bubbles but droplets of stout precipitating out of the gaseous head. Whilst all this was going on, the already spotless wooden counter was wiped and two new beermats placed before us. Our thirst and longing for the cool refreshing Guinness were being honed to a fine edge. At last the straight brimming glasses were placed before us with a deliberation and solemnity befitting the persona of our schoolmasterly host. I almost felt I should make the sign of the cross before lifting the glass to my lips. We drank deep.

I believe all those advertisements about Guinness giving you strength. I could feel the cool rich brew coursing through my body, reaching my swelling feet, my aching legs, my smarting face. It was to become a grand part of the walking day: that first pint of Guinness each evening; the further one had walked the more enjoyable it was. Today we had walked in bright sunshine for well over twenty miles.

Tony's forearms were red and sore, he was probably feeling as knackered as he'd ever felt in his life. The last five miles of our walk had been too much, and unnecessary. The previous several miles from Shillelagh to Clonegal were along a metalled road, often straight, so unexciting and rather a slog. The feeling that I was subjecting my old friend to a pointless ordeal returned. It was now that we began to discuss the possibility of cheating and taking the bus the next day. The map showed the road from Bunclody to New Ross, although it ran parallel to the line of the Blackstairs Mountains, to be long and rather featureless. Perhaps we could bus it there. I'd asked about a track along the ridge of the Blackstairs Mountains. This ridge forms the boundary between Counties Wexford and Carlow and someone thought there might be a boundary wall. This I suspected was only a wishful guess, though it would seem to be an obvious route for a long-distance footpath.

Bunclody is a pleasant town. It has a wide main street with a tree-lined stream running down its centre. We found a pub/hotel with an encouraging menu posted outside and thankfully sat down with a second pint and waited for our food – an inexpensive bar meal which turned out to be very good and excellent value. In the meantime an American family had entered and sat next to us. They consisted of a youngish couple and an older couple: mother, father, son and daughter-in-law, as we discovered. Father was a very large guy: his head was wreathed in long white hair from which sprang an enormous pair of spectacles. He had the appearance of an aged hippy, but a well-fed and well-heeled one. Mother was a plump, homely, middle-aged lady who spoke much more quietly than her spouse. Son was also tall but not gross, wore long hair and cowboy boots, and was very friendly but not in a pushy way. Daughter-in-law was big and attractive with a curvaceous figure that it was difficult to avoid constantly entering my field of vision, particularly as she was perched on a bar stool about a yard in front of me.

Father's name was Ted Rooney and he described himself as a poet. His wife was a reference librarian. As a former librarian and bookseller/publisher myself I felt we had something in common and relished the chat. Well, at first I did. Old Ted knew everyone – he was a dreadful name-dropper. His conversation, or monologue, consisted of a relentless barrage of names, places, and connections with other names and places, but little of any consequence. It was one against five and Old Ted won hands down. Tony and I finally extricated ourselves and returned to Deane's Hotel where we pretty soon crashed out. Had we not been so ready for sleep we would probably have been kept awake by the banging that was coming from adjacent rooms.

Thursday 21 May
Over breakfast the landlady told us that she was expecting 22 guests that evening, that half the rooms were still being fitted out. The chaotic state of the 'dining room' certainly bore out her story of unreadiness for the big hang-gliding weekend.

The most impressive building in Bunclody's main street is the Catholic church. It is new and spacious. I was to discover that, as in many communities in Ireland, the Catholic churches, especially the modern ones, are visually stunning, – they possess (the new buildings at least) an uncrowded and, yes, unadorned simplicity which provides a refreshing contrast to the often over-worked, over-decorated, clashing interiors and exteriors of domestic and commercial buildings, though the latter can often possess a peculiar charm. Inside this church was a small army of women cleaning and polishing in every corner.

A cluster of signs beside the town square informed us very precisely that New Ross was 24 and three quarter miles distant. On receiving this piece of information we decided to cheat: we would bus it and then walk, approximately half that distance, from New Ross to Arthurstown, where we planned to stay in the Youth Hostel. We alighted a luxurious bus which took a long way round, first down the Slaney valley to Enniscorthy, then back in a south-westerly direction to New Ross. The radio was switched on and we listened to a phone-in programme in which the forthcoming referendum, concerning the Single European Act and Ireland's relationship with the Common Market, was discussed at great length.

In New Ross, Tony purchased a long-sleeved white shirt to protect his sunburnt arms and a lightweight anorak to replace his heavy Barbour jacket; the latter he posted to his aunt in Dungarvan. New Ross has a curiously French atmosphere; this Frenchness was something I'd sensed already in Ireland and was to sense on more occasions.

Now we walked south, first close by the River Barrow which further on opened out into Waterford Harbour, then out of sight of the water, via Dunganstown - not a town at all but only a farm, the ancestral home of the US Kennedys (the John F Kennedy Memorial Park is nearby) – and various other hamlets, until we reached the road by Dunbrody Abbey. This much shorter day's walking, begun at 1 pm, was a delight. The day had started out fresh and overcast but, as the afternoon wore on, the sun came and went, through a broken sky. Our lane was lined with stone walls and trees, often beech, the banks clothed with ferns and bluebells. Mostly I walked ahead of Tony, about 20 yards or so, my reverie occasionally interrupted by a blast from his memo recorder as he played back a piece of verse he'd just composed. The fact that most of these pieces were composed on the hoof probably accounts for their plodding rhythm.

Dunbrody Abbey

At the junction with the main road near Dunbrody Abbey we stopped at a bar and asked for sandwiches and a pot of tea. For two rounds of meat sandwiches and three cups of tea each we were charged £1 – the landlady had surely made a loss on this transaction. I had noticed a casual attitude to charging for drinks and food: a total sum was sometimes rounded down to the nearest pound, but to charge only one pound for all this seemed not just casual but extremely generous.

The road crosses a creek where bladder-wrack clings to the stones at water-level. Dunbrody Abbey is a roofless ruin but impressive in its hill-top position. Farther on, as we crested a hill, a shaft of sunlight lit up Arthurstown, like a player on stage, and we could see the whole expanse of Waterford Harbour and the open sea beyond. Arthurstown is a small community with a bar and a few houses clustered near its jetty. The Youth Hostel is situated in a semi-derelict terrace of former coastguard cottages. The warden was a middle-aged lady who lived in a bungalow nearby. We checked in with her and accepted her offer of a cooked breakfast for the following morning. The hostel accommodation was basic, to say the least, but we had the luxury of a room to ourselves and a view across the bay, mine unimpeded by being seen through a broken window, propped open (as if extra ventilation were needed) by a framed, embroidered picture bearing the following message, headed MOTHER:

> Who is the one to whom we turn,
>   When all the world is grey,
> Who is the one for whom we yearn,
>   When we are far away?

We wandered into the village and entered the bar. There were several fellows drinking and one singing. A young man was sitting on a stool at the bar; to describe his utterances as singing from the heart would be a gross understatement. He'd obviously had a bit to drink and he was belting out his song, in slow motion, with all his soul, eyes tight shut, hands gripping his knees:

> Give me a breeze and a good rolling sea
> And I'll play me old squeeze box as we roll along
> With the wind in the riggings you'll sing us this song:
> 'Wrap me up in me oilskins and jumper
> And no more on the docks I'll be seen
> And just tell me old shipmates
> I'm taking a trip mates
> I'll see you some day on Fiddler's Green'

Fiddler's Green was followed by a ragged round of applause from his fellow drinkers, all equally inebriated, and an appeal for another song.

The last song was *The Mountains of Mourne*, the many verses of which recall the experience of an Irish emigrant in London, at first innocent and gullible, then sobered through experience in the great metropolis and finally expressing a longing to be home once again with his loved one:

> *So I'll wait for the wild rose that's waitin' for me*
> *Where the Mountains of Mourne sweep down to the sea.*

Tony knew all the words to this song; it had been his father's party piece. Indeed, I remember him singing it on occasions when he'd had a few drinks, once clutching a glass of whiskey sitting under the kitchen table.

We'd asked the warden about a place to eat. It was either this pub or an expensive seafood restaurant up the road in Ballyhack. Tony felt for his credit cards and we headed to the Neptune Restaurant. What a contrast to the village bar! As we sipped our aperitif and placed our order in a conservatory full of wicker furniture and pot plants we eavesdropped a conversation taking place between the proprietress and some representative from the Ministry of Tourism, or suchlike. It was all concerned with promoting tourism in the area.

This was a very up-front, up-market establishment, tastefully decorated, everything arranged with a designer's eye. We sat down to a Seafood Special and were presented with the innards of a host of local crustaceans, enough to have populated a considerable rockpool, all arranged on the plate like some abstract painting, in the style of *La Nouvelle Cuisine*. Tony was sufficiently inspired to photograph each course before he ate it: mushroom soup, green salad, seafood platter and plums in red wine. The French can sniff out good food and I wasn't surprised later to see a French truck outside waiting for the ferry to cross Waterford Harbour. I exchanged a *bon soir* with the driver of *Transports de Poissons*. Back in the village bar the singers were still at it. Other folk had arrived, including some women. Nobody minded the drunken uproar, indeed, it seemed to evoke a kind of amused tolerance. One of the lads, actually a middle-aged man with bleary eyes, the whites of which were as red as his face, told us that he wouldn't go home to face his wife, that he'd been on the piss for four days. I could believe it.

As we crossed the bay once again the sun was going down – it seemed to have been doing so for hours, creating the most spectacular effects

29

upon sea and sky. It was good to smell the sea and to know that it would be in view for the next couple of days. We waved to a fisherman returning to port and hauling in his nets; he stopped in order to wave back. The Irish are great wavers. We had soon learnt to so acknowledge every passing car on the road. In this case the wave was often restricted to an index finger slowly but steadily raised from the top of the steering wheel. Such friendly gestures seemed more common in parts of the country less frequented by tourists.

Friday 21 May
At Ballyhack a highly efficient ferry took us across Waterford Harbour to Passage East and from Wexford to County Waterford. The ferry was one of those floating stretches of road that vehicles drive on at one end and off the other. The wide estuary here narrows to about half a mile and the two opposing communities – Ballyhack and Passage East – would no doubt in the past have been twin sites of great strategic importance, defending the waterways to New Ross and Waterford City. Ballyhack is a neat nuclear village, its few houses and seafood restaurant dwarfed by the gaunt remains of a castle.

Some days later I picked up a beermat (in Ireland more accurately known as a drip-mat), one side of which depicted this same view of Ballyhack from the water, though its whereabouts was not indicated. On the reverse side was an invitation to write a story of not more than 300 words based on the illustration, for which Irish Distillers Limited were offering a £1,000 prize. The only stipulation was that 'naturally, the story must include a reference to Power's Gold Label Whiskey and that you must be at least 18 years of age.' I guess you have to be 18 to write about booze as well as to imbibe it.

The day was overcast and rather dull as we turned left at Passage East, southwards, along a lane that followed the shore. A brief shower here was to be the only rain we encountered until our last day in Dublin. The most colourful objects hereabouts are the occasional roadside pumps cheerfully painted blue and white, the Waterford colours. We did try the pumps from time to time on our walk; most worked and the water from them was usually clear and sweet-tasting, although they cannot be much used today.

This lane, with its views across Waterford Harbour, was lined with bungalows, the one feature of Ireland which we found even more ubiquitous than the yellow-flowering gorse. It's curious that a country with so much dereliction in the form of abandoned buildings: great houses, churches, abbeys, castles, but, most of all and most poignantly, your humble cottages, is also a country with widespread and ever-present evidence of new building which, in the country at least, is almost exclusively in the shape of the bungalow.

Official census figures show that Ireland's population declined from over eight million in 1841 to well under five million 50 years later, both as a result of death from starvation during the Great Famine and from sustained high levels of emigration, a phenomenon which is a continuing fact of Irish life. Large numbers of folk left after the Second World War and through the 1960s until Ireland joined the European Economic Community (1973). Then this small island nation lying on the fringe of Europe had access to a much larger market for its agricultural produce, in particular beef and dairy produce. Subsidies via the Common Agricultural Policy poured into the pockets of all but the smallest farmers throughout the country, although the traditionally impoverished west, with the poorest farming land, came off worst as usual.

A relatively poor country with low wage rates and access to the European market attracted capital from overseas, including the USA and Japan, and new factories were built. The rate of emigration dropped sharply and many Irish people who had been living and working in England began to drift back home. By the mid-1980s, with an adverse economic climate internationally, things have taken a turn for the worse. Government spending on the care services and infrastructure of the country grew and grew during the good times, and borrowing increased by such a large measure that Ireland now has one of the highest per capita debts in the world.

Emigration is again on the increase and has become a political issue. In many ways this traditional escape route from Ireland's troubles only compounds the problem: the young and able and economically active head overseas, leaving the very young and old who, whilst perhaps gaining the benefit of monies sent home from relatives abroad, will also be to some extent dependent upon the state.

A month or two before we arrived in Ireland, a General Election had been held in which the *Fine Gael* had been defeated and *Fianna Fail* elected to power, though only just. I had been following the campaign in the British media and, for the life of me, could find incredibly little difference between the two parties in terms of policy – certainly both agreed Ireland was in an economic mess and something needed to be done about it – but a world of difference between the styles of the leaders: Garret FitzGerald - softly spoken, academic, almost reluctant, the leader of *Fine Gael* and Charles (Charlie to his supporters) Haughey – the immodest, colourful and pugnacious chief of *Fianna Fail*. Haughey it was who promised, during the campaign, no cuts in the health service and lots of other things the voters wanted to hear but now, only weeks later, it was Haughey and his ruling party who were enacting the most drastic cuts in public services the country had ever seen. Whenever domestic politics came up in conversation with the folk we met the main impression I got was one of overwhelming cynicism, with barely a good word uttered for the new Taoiseach (Prime Minister), or anyone else in politics for that matter. I suppose this is not so different from England.

A ruined cottage and a new bungalow

But there remain the bungalows – the one lasting reminder of the prosperity which accession to the EEC has brought Ireland. Everywhere one sees abandoned homes, especially in Wicklow and further west, but everywhere too one is forced eyeball to casement window with spanking new houses, all single storey, usually built on a simple rectangular plan with a gabled roof, occasionally hipped, of concrete blocks and mortar, the walls rendered and painted, sometimes with a whimsical sculpting performed by the plasterer before the concrete had hardened. Sometimes too a section of exterior wall exhibits a panel of multicoloured bricks arranged in a geometrical pattern, or a mass of slate cemented together to form a 'crazy' pattern. Other extras might include a Moorish arch or an ornate pair of gateposts surmounted by gilded eagles or plaster dogs, rather according to *Dallas*.

In New Ross I had leafed through a magazine entitled *Bungalow Bliss* which gave construction plans and ideas for fitting out and decoration. It does seem that the prevailing notion of bliss in Ireland today is a pristine bungalow in the country. It is so for many people in England too, though the English are perhaps more likely to settle for a house in a neat row of similar in some suburban street than for a single dwelling on a large plot of land in some wild and isolated location – perhaps through choice as well as financial necessity. But in England many people would prefer the old country cottage, preferably stone-built and thatched, with wooden beams and roses round the door. They would jump at a chance to restore one of the thousands of such derelict properties to be found in the Irish countryside. But here such a 'charming country cottage in need of modernisation' - to use estate agent's jargon – seems never to be touched but only left to fall down in its own sweet time. One often sees these rotting shells only yards from the new bungalow – as though the owners want to keep the old home as a reminder of their poverty-stricken past and of their new-found prosperity.

It is obviously good news that so many Irish people are living in decent houses and enjoying much improved living conditions. A recent book entitled *A Fair Day: Photographs from the West of Ireland* (Promenade Press, 1984) devotes a section to pictures of new bungalows, some Dallas-like, others more modest. The author Fintan O'Toole introduces his commentary by saying that 'to build a house is the ultimate declaration of intent to stay put, of confidence in the future', a marked contrast to the emigration and subsequent dereliction of the recent past. It is to be hoped that such confidence holds and that we don't see a whole new era of abandoned homes in Ireland. Meanwhile, all power to those voices warning of the gobbling up of the beautiful Irish countryside by this great rash of new bungalows and advocating tighter controls to regulate such development.

Somewhere a few miles south of Passage East we took a wrong turn and emerged onto the main road from Waterford to the airport at

Dunmore East, thereby missing the lane which climbed a hill to an intriguingly named Fairybush Crossroads. Instead we walked beside Belle Lake, a body of water about a mile long, and regained our lane further on. Now we descended to the head of a creek which led to Back Strand, a considerable lagoon behind the sand bar reaching out from Tramore which all but cuts off this area from the sea. I had hoped to cross the inlet to reach the bar and thereby the seaside town of Tramore. The roadside pub here was shut. As Tony attempted to outbark the St Bernard guard dog and I deliberated the route, the owners drove up and opened the bar.

We were informed that there was a ferry across but it didn't operate until June and the sinking sand should not be negotiated on foot. We were then advised to take the road; I could see from the map that this was a long way round and reckoned we could walk along the creek and then along the edge of Back Strand. When we set out the sky had cleared and it was a splendid day. The tide was brimming as we picked our way across the sand and slaty rock of the shore. There were tufts of pink thrift and many colourful shelduck. The scene was marred only by the shocking amount of rubbish, mostly indestructible plastic detritus, containers of washing up liquid predominating. I picked up a battered book; it was *Robinson Crusoe*, which seemed appropriate.

The way along the shoreline soon became difficult and we headed up to the fields: from here we had an unimpeded view towards Tramore, its church tower beckoning us onward. Our route, unfortunately, was not so unimpeded; we had to climb banks and scramble through hedges between several field boundaries. When much closer we came to a deep flooded inlet and were forced to retrace our steps and approach the town by the main road. Here a huge rat crossed my path and disappeared down a hole in the grass verge.

I caught up with a small boy who, apropos of nothing, told me that he was eight years old with an Irish mother and an English father and had spent the first half of his life in England. He pointed out his very nice house and said he preferred Ireland because there was 'more space to play'. His hobby was birdwatching – he had spotted 115 species but considered egg-collecting unacceptable. He was off delivering leaflets to his neighbours which urged them to vote YES in the coming referendum in which voters were being asked to decide on the Single European Act – the question as we understood it was that of Irish neutrality.

Our lack of success in quickly reaching Tramore was rather

frustrating and we were pleased finally to arrive. Tony knew the town from holidays in the past. It has a marvellous situation and possesses a perfect, south-facing beach, or strand, as beaches are known in Ireland. We were desperate for some refreshment by this time and almost as desperate for money. It was Friday and already past bank closing time. I managed to find a bank and rang the bell. I was scrutinised from a peephole and spoken to through a crack in the bolted door. When the clerk was convinced he was not about to be raided I was allowed in and the door locked behind me. I was most courteously dealt with and left wondering whether the rules could be bent so easily in England.

We sat down to a pot of tea and sandwiches in a wonderfully atmospheric bar. It was a cavern of a place, I guess purpose-built for the tourists, with full-size snooker tables and benches to seat hundreds. I will always find alluring the prospect of green baize illuminated from overhead and the gentle clunk of billiard balls. I suppose there's something womb-like about the hushed, darkened surroundings. Not that this bar was very hushed, – while we sat sipping our tea we were entertained to a selection of hits from the early sixties: Duane Eddy played *Peter Gunn* and *Forty Miles of Bad Road*, and Anthony Newley sang a succession of his old hits. These were pumped through the loudspeakers in the ceiling, at considerable volume. You become accustomed to such blatant contrasts in Ireland.

What may have been a cliff path was indicated as we walked uphill out of Tramore. No publicity is given to coastal footpaths in Ireland so perhaps none exist. Such a route here would have been a wonderful bonus and actually the most direct way to Annestown, next stop along the coast. I couldn't persuade Tony to attempt such a route and it was just as well we didn't – the half inch map which I later acquired shows absolutely no evidence of a coastal footpath. Several miles further on where the lane takes an inconvenient turn inland I enquired further – the request for information about a coastpath elicited only directions along the lane to the main road. The very concept of a path seems not to exist in the minds of the Irish. People don't walk, except when they have to. Car ownership is probably as widespread as it is in Britain. I suppose a car is essential in a rural society where bus services are limited and public transport expensive.

Footpaths do exist, however, but are not indicated on maps, even large-scale ones. Perhaps this is not simply because they are not much used, but also because, in Ireland, there are no rights of way. Not that this prevents one from walking overland. Irish farmers and landowners seem to have a pretty relaxed attitude to such 'trespass', and there is so much uncultivated land anyway, especially in the most scenic parts of the country. Yet without a network of footpaths, one has to take a chance on not finding obstacles such as rivers and bogs and thick undergrowth. Soon after I made this enquiry I saw a stile in the hedgerow which led across a small field to a stile on the far side to rejoin the lane. This route for pedestrians cut a corner where the lane made a hairpin bend. I was often to see stiles which obviously heralded field paths but there was not once a signpost; one concludes that these ways are only known and used by locals.

The Wicklow Way, Ireland's first official long-distance footpath, leads the walker through some very impressive scenery but is entirely a modern creation: a hotchpotch of lanes, forest tracks and military road. It lacks the historical integrity of an ancient track like the Ridgeway in southern England or the topographical significance of the Pennine Way. The Wicklow Way zigzags about to take in the best of the mountain scenery but, because of this eccentricity and in the absence of comprehensive signposting, needs constant attention – a necessity which detracts from the enjoyment of the walking and seeing. There must surely be enormous potential for both long-distance and local walking in Ireland, a relatively quiet and sparsely populated land with so much in the countryside to interest walkers.

We crossed a bridge over a river near sea-level and climbed up the hill to Annestown. It was seven o'clock and we were tired and rather cold. We could not find digs or even a bar. We bought our supper in the shop where we were told that Annestown was surely the only place in Ireland without a bar. We sat on a bench beside the village pump and ate our uncooked fare, becoming even colder. Opposite was a Protestant church; we could not see a Catholic church – was this the reason that Annestown was a town without beer? Tony was weakening in anticipation of seeing his aunt and had telephoned her before we ate. They would drive out to meet us and take us four or five miles Dungarvan-wards to Bunmahon where we would have a drink and find a place to stay. We would walk the remaining 15 miles to Dungarvan the following day.

We spent the night in a particularly impressive bungalow on a rise with views out to sea; before that we enjoyed a few pints and a chat with Tony's aunt Eileen, her husband Ned and the few people at the bar. The landlady was a resourceful seeming lady, very old and wearing a rugby striped sweater. When I was buying a round a fellow at the bar asked,

'Are you walking?'

'Yes,' says I.

'Oh, on bikes', says your man.

How could we be walking on bikes?

'No, walking', I confirmed.

'You're hitching?' says he.

'No, walking!'

Evidently a local, I asked this guy about a coastpath for the next day's walking but was again referred to the road. It's a shame, for I'm sure this Waterford coastline deserves a path. I had been imagining one for months before as I studied the maps in planning the walk, so was a little disappointed not to find one.

Saturday 22 May

From Bunmahon, with the prospect of a leisurely weekend in Dungarvan, we set out the next day at a brisk pace through Stradbally and on past the disused railway viaduct at Ballyvoyle. Even in the absence of a coast path, this was a lovely and enjoyable few miles. Walking above the narrow valley towards the sea the road bears right and follows a direct, low-lying and slightly tedious course to Dungarvan. Coastwards, to our left, was Clonea Castle and Bay. The road follows the line of the old railway. Tony's grandfather it was who came to live in Dungarvan to work on the railway. By now my companion was musing nostalgically upon the times as a child when he and his family rode on the train from Rosslare all the way to Dungarvan where they would wave to their grandparents in their garden while steaming through. Thus inspired, we decided to climb onto the track and follow this into town. Strangely, although the line was long disused, the rails were still laid (though well-rusted) and, more oddly, the line took a sharp and uncorrected left hand turn.

After one and a half miles thus we found ourselves, not in Dungarvan, as we had expected, but at a monstrous derelict site, a great contemporary structure which apparently had some industrial or manufacturing function. We learned later that this was an abandoned bauxite processing plant. A branch line had been maintained to transport the ore from Kilkenny and, although the plant had since closed down, the rails had not been lifted. More dereliction, but this time of more modern origin, much larger scale than cottages or even castles and not nearly as picturesque. A well-kept but forbidden drive led beside the works to a lighthouse at Ballynacourty Point where we saw through a gate in the walled enclosure below the lighthouse across the wide expanse of Dungarvan Harbour to the town and the Drum Hills and the bastion of Helvick Head which shelters the harbour from the prevailing south-westerlies.

When we realised the error of our ways we followed the road, quiet enough, as always, first beside Dungarvan Golf Links and then directly beside the shallow, brimming inlet to reach the rail bridge, now a pedestrian way, across a creek. This detour added some interest and about three miles to the indicated 15 from Bunmahon to Dungarvan. It was four o'clock when we found Tony's aunt's house in a modern estate of semis in Abbeyside, once a separate settlement but now really a suburb of Dungarvan. Another set of road and rail bridges cross the River Colligan to join the two places.

After changing my footwear I wandered into Dungarvan, leaving Tony to his aunt and her family, and visited the bookshop and a chemist and bought some postcards to send home. Dungarvan is quite a bustling place – there are a great many shops, a large number of which line the four sides of Grattan Square, in what is really a small town.

I noticed the building materials in use here: dark red sandstone, from the Old Red Sandstone formation from which the bulk of all the mountain systems in south-west Ireland are made. Dungarvan Quay and many of the now largely disused warehouses are built of pale grey limestone – the Carboniferous Limestone which is often exposed in the folds of the mountains in this region of Ireland. Both are good, compact rocks which can be shaped to form solid, durable building blocks. This combination of red sandstone and pale grey limestone is reminiscent of the Mendip Hills of Somerset: here the same formations form the bedrock, the same rocks are used for building and, in fact, the hills of both regions owe their origin to the Armorican orogenesis, or mountain-building period, and the ridges and valleys have an east-west alignment. These terrestrial upheavals took place around 300 million years ago and once massive mountains have been worn down to mere stumps, the finishing touches to their present appearance carried out during the last Ice Age. Some summits rise to over 2,000 feet and a few, further west in the peaks beyond Killarney, to over 3,000 feet.

The Carboniferous Limestone is also the formation which gives rise to The Burren, that great naked limestone pavement in County Clare, and forms the bedrock of a great deal of Central Ireland. Certainly this island does not possess the geological diversity of mainland Britain, where rocks of practically every geological period are represented and where the repeated crumpling and cracking of the earth's crust has given rise to an amazingly varied landscape, and also to certain rich mineral deposits which have been of the greatest importance in Britain's development. A tiny patch of Cretaceous Chalk near Killarney and some Tertiary clays in Tipperary suggest that these formations were once widespread across Ireland but that the forces of erosion over hundreds of millions of years have stripped the landscape of many potentially useful rocks.

One example is the absence of flint (no chalk), so important to the economy of Stone Age man. The Jurassic freestones, which form the limestone belt reaching across England from the south-west to the north-east, is entirely absent. These omissions have not only deprived Ireland of a superb building stone and so impoverished vernacular architecture, but have also denied the country the valuable ironstones which formed an essential ingredient of Britain's industrial revolution. Another mineral in short supply, of course, is coal; although Ireland has, in abundance, limestone from the Carboniferous period, it does not have the material from which that geological period is named. In fact there is a little coal around Kilkenny, – pits were once worked here but no longer.

Of the most coveted resource of the late twentieth century, oil, Ireland has thus far found none, though a gas field off the coast of Cork is exploited. Ireland does have enormous quantities of peat, a low-grade fuel maybe, but one which the Irish use extensively both for the domestic fire and boiler and also in full-scale power stations, and this is one technology in which they are world leaders.

I might have been able to find out more about the geology of the district in the town's library and museum, an attractive building recently converted from one of the old warehouses near the quay. Unfortunately, I'd left it a bit late after chatting to the assistants in the bookshop and chemist's. I strolled back across the bridge where I was alarmed to see the river no longer flowing seawards but the sea flowing landwards .... there seems to be a considerable rise and fall of the tide at this point. I continued along the track of the old railway, now used as a convenient walkway from Dungarvan to Abbeyside.

That evening Ned and Eileen drove us out to Helvick Head – such a

Norse-sounding name. Before we reached that promontory we drove down to a couple of coves with small quays jutting out to sea. One was crammed with small local fishing vessels, some of which bore black flags. It was explained to us that these fishermen had been convicted for using nets with an illegally fine mesh in order to catch salmon. They insisted that Spanish vessels were also using such nets, hence the protest.

The Drum Hills behind us harbour a tiny enclave of Gaelic speaking Irish folk, and is known as *An Rinn*, a place far removed from the larger *Gaeltacht* districts to the west and north. This survival is perhaps the more surprising in being so near a once considerable port, with all its cosmopolitan influences. There is a college here where people come to learn Gaelic. The Irish Government has long encouraged the use of the native tongue and it is a compulsory part of the school curriculum; every child is expected to achieve a certain standard and access to many jobs in the public sector is dependent upon a knowledge of Gaelic. To an Englishman the written language looks as foreign and difficult as Polish, using a surfeit of g's and h's where Polish is scattered with c's and z's. We did occasionally hear the language being used – not in *An Rinn*, but once or twice in Kerry in a natural everyday fashion, and once on the radio. That radio broadcast was certainly attractive sounding; it reminded me most forcibly of Welsh – totally incomprehensible but soft and lilting and expressive.

Unlike Counties Wexford and Wicklow, the road signs in Waterford are bilingual - Gaelic first, English second, though, with the exception of *An Rinn*, Waterford seemed to be a comparatively anglicised part of Ireland. To confuse the issue further, the newer roadsigns give distances in kilometres rather than miles; in a Wicklow forest I had seen specimen trees bearing notices giving their height in feet and their volume in cubic metres. I guess all this confusion is symptomatic of Ireland's search for her true identity in the modern world with the sometimes conflicting traditions of Ireland, England, America and now, increasingly, the European Community all playing a part.

We stopped at a couple of pubs; at the second there was a band, a group of mainly young people sitting informally on stools in the middle of the bar and all in high spirits and enjoying themselves immensely. They romped through number after number. Ned asked me which was my favourite Irish song; I thought of *Fiddlers Green*, the song which we'd heard in the bar in Arthurstown and which had been going through my mind for several days. The band played it, dedicating it to

Tony and Roger who had walked from Dublin 'today'. An old man was playing the *bodhrán*, the native Irish drum, and fitted in beautifully with the guitars, mandolin, penny whistle and accordion, the last in the expert hands of a 15 year old girl, as we found out later.

Tony was enjoying every minute of this. Leaning forward on his seat, I could see he was itching to grab a guitar and join in. Tony is a dedicated musician, a composer of music as well as a player. Apart from the little session in Knockananna he'd not got his hands on an instrument and was visibly suffering withdrawal symptoms. We'd been at secondary school together from 1956 to 1961. We'd not become friendly until the last couple of years – he was a quiet lad who kept himself to himself and didn't much join up with other boys.

In the fourth year a few of us had produced a newspaper dedicated to the all-important subject of pop music. We named it *Vox Musicae,* no doubt to impress the teachers and lend it an air of respectability; without asking permission we pinned it up on a noticeboard at the back of the classroom. The teachers were utterly perplexed; the Latin master, after being drawn to it by its title, turned away in disgust. Pretty soon *Vox Musicae* was banned from school premises.

Soon after this Tony and I got together. We both had guitars and wanted to be our own pop group. I was unmusical to the extent of being tested for tone-deafness at Junior School (I passed) but Tony had natural musical talent. I learned a few chords, sufficient to provide a rhythm guitar backing to Tony's much more skilled lead guitar. Others joined us and we got a group going. It consisted of the usual line-up for 1961: lead, rhythm and bass guitar, drums and vocalist (never called a singer!) When we left school at the end of the fifth year the group reformed with more able personnel but Tony and I remained as lead and rhythm guitar. An old friend of mine drove us to gigs in his van. I can't claim we were ever much good but we had some memorable sessions and it was great fun – about the nearest I ever got to team-work.

Sunday 23 May

The Sabbath dawned and we were both to go to Mass: 11.30am in The Friary Church (founded in the twelfth century by the Austin Friars who had been driven into the hills at the time of the Penal Laws but had eventully returned to Dungarvan and built their present church *c.* 1820) had been chosen for us. We arrived early – necessary in order to secure a seat. This was just an ordinary Sunday but the church was packed to bursting, even the balcony was full. I should say the average age of the congregation could not have been much over 25; there were crowds of children and an especially high proportion of teenagers.

There was a large choir, strumming guitars, and two women to read the lessons - the whole performance was slick and well-rehearsed. The word performance came to mind because this is what the proceedings seemed to constitute: a great spectacle, but an event lacking spontaneity or any element of surprise. The choir and guitar strummers and women readers played their part but there seemed no opportunity for the packed congregation to make a contribution, except simply to be there. Yet I suppose this is true of most services in other churches and denominations where there is no opportunity for individual ministry.

The altar was an edifice constructed of finely worked white marble with gilt decoration topped with brass candlesticks: all was bright and shining. Before mass began the altar boys and other helpers scuttled around lighting candles and preparing for the event. There was a great air of expectancy as the priest entered. He wore a slightly smug air. Apparently a visiting cleric, he attempted a lighthearted approach by introducing himself as a Donegal man from Limerick and added that he would be praying for his own football team later in the year, not with the Dungarvan supporters. None of this elicited any audible or visible response, I wondered what would have happened if it had. After the pleasantries came the message: we were urged to come to mass daily during the pre-Pentecost Solemn Novena.

The sermon concerned Christ's spirit, the Holy Spirit, which was fitting to this pre-Pentecost time. To me his language was very mechanistic – too much received theology and dogma, too little original thought and feeling to convince or inspire. He repeated his message several times: 'Every member of every family to attend mass every day over this nine day period, so that, through prayer, an island of reconciliation and peace will be created around Dungarvan during this period in this disturbed world.' I would not dispute the worth and power of prayer; it seems to me an essential basis of the Christian life, but it is surely a basis, a springboard for action. I asked myself whether such compulsive church attendance was such a springboard, an end in itself or merely a diversion.

I don't mean to be cynical. It was a humbling and impressive experience to see such a large body of people worshipping in such sincerity. Church-going has surely survived in Ireland to a far greater degree than in almost any other country in the world; it is the cornerstone of many people's lives, an anchor, a certainty. When I got married in 1970 I hadn't practised my faith for many years. My wife-to-be wanted to be married in church so I felt it was time for a reconciliation. I attended mass locally and was moved at the sight of people going forward to receive Holy Communion. The prone kneeling position, the tongue extended for the host, the humble and accepting attitude of the participants: all this impressed me deeply.

Here in Dungarvan practically the entire congregation received the Blessed Sacrament. Several other priests emerged to help dole out the host. The faith of the people could not be denied but the priests, slightly sinister in their black robes, seemed too safe, too certain, their authority unquestioned. And why should they doubt their authority when they are supported by such large, faithful congregations? Notices in support of Solemn Novena were given out at the end of mass and people were urged to place them in their windows. We saw scores of them so displayed, like election posters.

There were also leaflets being distributed by the representatives of the National Rosary Campaign urging folk to vote NO to the Single European Act in the coming referendum in order 'to retain the power to protect our unborn, our families, our youth, our culture and our country. We must again be a light to the nations.' For the supporters of this movement the issue at stake was not a narrow political one concerning some nicety of the Irish Constitution but one which affected the life of the nation and, above all, basic moral principles. That the church in Ireland sees itself as the guardian of the people against the threats of a hostile world is clear enough but that last phrase, 'We must again be a light to the nations', indicates an awareness of the missionary role of the church, and of Ireland as Catholic nation. This seemed to hark back to Irland's Golden Age which was contemporary with England's Dark Age, when Ireland kept the flame of Christianity burning and its sons went forth to convert the rest of Europe. The priest had exhorted his congregation to vote but had not told them whether to vote YES or NO.

After Sunday dinner in Abbeyside Tony and I walked into Dungarvan. It was a pleasant afternoon and it was pleasant indeed to stroll hither and thither, exploring back streets, entering churches, to take one's time and follow one's nose, rather than to be marching from point A some 20 miles or so to point B.

The Parish Church was even bigger and more impressive than the one we had attended in the morning. Like all Irish churches it was beautifully kept (a contrast to all the neglected Catholic churches I had seen in France in recent years) and contained all those essential elements of Roman Catholicism: candles, confessionals, the Stations of the Cross, the bookstall full of booklets dealing with topical issues from a Catholic viewpoint. I purchased one dealing with *Cults, Sects and New Religious Groups* which dealt with the onslaught of the Moonies, etc., the priest-author admitting to a 'spiritual malnutrition behind the impressive Church practice in Ireland.' I felt this critique was fair and balanced and, in this respect, rather different to some of those pamphlets issued by the Catholic Truth Society when I was at school. One I still possess concerning nuclear war I find a blatant apology for weapons of mass destruction and covered in my indignant red ink of thirty years ago.

The church notice board exhibited a whole range of special interest groups: Alcoholics Anomynous, Natural Birth Control, Mental Health, Charismatic Renewal. The English-looking Protestant church was, predictably, locked. There was one Sunday Service given by a vicar who lived miles away in Lismore. There were a few recent graves and the stones bore a mixture of English and Irish names. Dungarvan on this Sunday afternoon was full of teenagers – they were wholesome youngsters and were very friendly and curious, especially the girls. And not at all threatening, like many kids of a similar age in England. Indeed the children in Ireland are a constant delight – they appear not to have been warned against speaking to strange adults – in place of fear is a refreshing friendliness and openness.

The weekend in Abbeyside had rested, refreshed, informed and entertained. I felt too I'd made new friends and begun to understand another facet of Tony's life in meeting his aunt and her family. Our first week had been spent walking most of the way from Dublin to Dungarvan. During this second week we intended to reach the Kerry coast but were convinced that we should not overdo the walking too much in order to say we had walked every inch of the way. I had originally intended to take three weeks to cover this long walk as I had when I walked 380 plus miles from London to Land's End in 1984. When Tony had said he'd join me in Ireland we had to take fewer days so that he shouldn't use up too much of his annual holiday allowance. I had whittled my projected route down to a minimum number of miles but they weren't sufficiently few that we could cover them in the time without it being rather a strain. After all we were each 42 years old and not the fittest of men. As I've said, Tony was entirely new to walking, and whilst he had shown he was not one to give up easily, I didn't want him dicing with death through exhaustion as he'd done on Day 1 in the Wicklow Mountains. We figured we'd walk this day the 18 or so miles to Lismore and then bus it to Cork.

Monday 24 May
To say that I felt eager anticipation as we set out from Abbeyside that Monday morning would be an understatement. The weather still held fair, it was a breezy, billowy sort of day – perfect for walking. Ned had given us a bottle of poteen as a parting gift. We had tried this the night before and found it like liquid fire. It was no small amount but a glass litre bottle full of the stuff. We were never going to drink this and it was a heavy item to carry. We decided to keep a small amount but to ditch the remainder – it ended in the flower bed outside Dungarvan Post Office. We bought two small bottles of soft drink and filled them with the remains so that we might keep a morsel of the potent brew. Mine still lurks in our drinks cupboard at home.

We walked out of Dungarvan, on our third day here now remarkably familiar. At last I had acquired some larger scale maps – half inch to the mile, and these made navigation much simpler and more certain. We sought out a minor road, actually a dirt track. This ran, like a towpath, for two miles beside the canalised River Brickey which drained the north-facing slopes of the Drum Hills. As we regained the metalled road we came close to a ruined church on a hillock and I was reminded of some similar remains on the Somerset levels. We crossed the Finisk River which flows west to join the grand River Blackwater a mile or two south of Cappoquin.

I am used to solitary walking, so spending day after day on the road in the company of another was a new experience. Tony was an old friend and a close one; in some ways we had shared similar experiences but in many ways had led quite different lives. He'd married in 1968, myself in 1970. I'm sure we'd both agree that our closest friends were our wives. We had gone to the same Roman Catholic Grammar School, given up church-going soon after we'd left but both found our ways back to some form of Christianity.

My wife and I had become interested in Quakerism in the mid-1970s and had eventually joined the Society of Friends in the early 1980s. I was drawn to Quakerism because, although firmly a part of the Christian tradition, it seems to have stripped away all the man-made superstructure and unnecessary ritual of mainstream Christianity, whether Catholic or Protestant, and to concentrate on the bare essentials. Rejected not only are the marble altars and brass candlesticks, but also the priests and the literal acceptance of every word in the Bible. Other positive attractions of Quakerism are the peace witness and the exemplary Christian lives of many individual Friends.

Tony had remained outside the church until later than me, though not much later. The loss of both his parents by the age of 21 had been a painful experience. If God was so vindictive, why should He be acknowledged?, he'd asked himself. Yet eventually Tony had become interested in Christian worship once again and began to attend a Baptist church. A crisis in his personal life at this time challenged his moral and religious beliefs. The result was a Road to Damascus conviction from which he does not seem to have wavered, so I guess it must have been the genuine article. He was, at first, a little hard to bear but has mellowed and, thankfully, has not lost his left-wing sympathies, nor does he hold that politics are irrelevant, like so many 'born again' Christians. I almost envy him his faith. His God is a personal God, he has experienced the gifts of the spirit and even prays to his God in tongues! I fear that I am a good way behind in my Christian development, or perhaps on a separate track altogether.

Such contrasting perceptions certainly provided opportunities for some productive and interesting conversation. Apart from this walk across Ireland, Tony and I usually see each other about two or three times a year, usually accompanied by our wives and youngest children, so there's hardly time for philosophical discourse, let alone the chance of a quiet pint together. The walk provided hour after hour – we began in Wicklow by discussing the British General Election and the State of the World, serious matters indeed.

Maybe I had imparted a little of my joy in the natural world; Tony would look at me in amazement when I gave a name to some lowly plant in the hedgebank. I had somehow been on top during the first week – me the seasoned walker leading the way, jollying him along. Though I cannot say I ever sought his guidance, I had always respected Tony's experience in matters of family and business, and I greatly admired his creative ability, his religious faith, his sense of humour. This second week we were again equal – I suppose because we'd decided not to overdo the walking but simply to enjoy ourselves, and Tony now had a week's solid tramping under his belt. We had some great conversations, often giving rise to hearty laughter, and these encounters, whilst trekking along unknown Irish lanes, will probably remain the sweetest memory of our Irish jaunt.

Tony had often said that although he was born and lived in England it was in Ireland that he truly felt at home. London is the great melting pot of the British Isles – my own forbears had been drawn by the promise of economic betterment, my mother from Jersey in the Channel Islands in the 1930s and my father's parents from South Wales in the 1890s. I am in fact no more English than Tony and the fact that we'd both attended a school for Roman Catholics set us somewhat apart from the mainstream. The majority of the boys there were of Irish descent and a substantial minority of East European, mainly Polish, origin. I suppose I feel English; I certainly love the land of England, but have always been turned off by any form of nationalism or, indeed, patriotism. But, perversely perhaps, I can appreciate these feelings in the Irish or any people which is, or has been, for so much of its recent history, the underdog.

My father unquestioningly supported the underdog, right or wrong (can the underdog be wrong?), and I have imbibed this attitude. My Catholicism, such as it is, or was, came from my mother: Jersey is a hotchpotch of denominations, with Catholicism, Protestantism and Methodism claiming about equal shares of the population. The old man was brought up chapel, Welsh Presbyterian in fact. His father was teetotal and strict rules applied to one's behaviour, especially on the Sabbath. He did not practise his religion but it had left its mark. I remember that we were given a day off school when John XXIII was made Pope in 1958. I was watching the long drawn out ceremony on television when Dad muttered, 'What a load of mumbo-jumbo' - this elaborate ritual being a far cry from his plain chapel origins.

As a child I had once gone with him to a Welsh chapel in Hammersmith to which he subscribed but which he rarely attended. He was very deaf and couldn't follow the all-important singing. I recall the stark chapel interior and the many people who sang with real conviction and great enjoyment, their faces lit up with the fervour of it all. One of Dad's favourite memories was of childhood holidays in Wales where, after evening chapel, the congregation would gather on the beach and sing their hearts out praising God, to the accompaniment of the wind and the waves.

'It fairly made the hairs stand up on the back of your neck, son', he'd always say.

At my local Catholic church, which I attended regularly with my mother, I recall the ornate plasterwork and decoration, the paintings and statues, the fine vestments and sickly incense, fascinating but also slightly oppressive.

Did Tony now feel so much at home in Ireland? This eccentric way of discovering the country, on foot, without his immediate family, seemed to be having a cathartic effect; he'd nurtured a particular image of his long dead father which was now perhaps undergoing revision.

Former grandeur

We'd covered the 13 or 14 miles to Cappoquin before the banks closed. This small, one-street town, with such a musical sounding name, lies at the southern foot of the Knockmealdown Mountains on a bend of the River Blackwater. The town was deadly quiet with not a soul in sight. After calling at the bank we found a bar and partook of our now customary afternoon tea and sandwiches. Further down the street we passed the Protestant church, a neat looking building standing in its churchyard and looking very English; unfortunately the door was locked. We planned to take the road on the south bank of the river to reach Lismore, this road was unnumbered on the map and would, we guessed, prove the quieter route.

Pausing on the bridge we had a fine view back over the town. The grey Protestant church stood out and nearby was the pale-coloured belfry and facade of the Catholic church, less ancient perhaps but, no doubt, better used. The railway bridge on the far side of the river's 90 degree bend is a curiosity. It begins as a traditional masonry structure and is then built of steel. I wondered if this was the result of partial destruction and rebuilding during the struggles of 1921. No boats were visible here, save one old man rowing a large vessel up-river. The mouth of the Blackwater lies about 15 miles to the south, at Youghal; this river must surely have once been a busy commercial waterway. There were what appeared to be the remains of some riverside warehouses – one bore the faded latters 'Cappoquin Bacon Factory'.

A glance at any map of southern Ireland will reveal the long River Blackwater; rising on the Cork/Kerry border the Blackwater flows due east, without deviation, from Rathmore for 60 miles via Mallow, Fermoy and Lismore to Cappoquin where, with the utmost perversity, it turns through 90 degrees, then pierces a high ridge to reach the sea at Youghal. The valley of the Blackwater, but not the river, continues eastwards to Dungarvan. As the geologists have pointed out, such eccentric behaviour must indicate that the present course of the Blackwater represents an earlier drainage pattern which has been superimposed upon the present, considerably eroded landscape.

A further four or five miles took us to Lismore. The path did not stick close to the river bank but we did once or twice meet the Blackwater when we gazed across and up and down its deep, dark, gently flowing waters to tree-fringed banks. We climbed slightly before entering Lismore and gained views across the foothills of the Knockmealdowns to the peaks beyond: Mount Knockmealdown, at 2,609 feet, had its head in the clouds. One peak in close proximity was the slender, piercing spire of the Protestant Cathedral. At the head of Lismore's main street we found a rather brash looking hotel. What appeared to be a jaunting car was perched on a ledge at first floor level and the façade was hung with wagon wheels; all was painted red and white. The hotel declared its identity as Terry's in a sign of fat italic script identical to that of Terry's Chocolate of York, England.

We checked in here (B & B was remarkably cheap) and sat supping Guinness to regain our strength. A portly, prosperous looking, English-sounding, middle-aged guy at the bar was saying he would be voting NO in the coming referendum. A younger man said he didn't care if he had a nuclear reactor in his back garden so long as he had a job (this implied that he would be voting YES). The whole argument

AIJ—D

seemed to resolve itself between the Realists and the Idealists, those who were for economic advance and the EEC – YESes, and those on the left and right who objected on the grounds of some principle – the sanctity of the family, Irish neutrality, refusal to accept nuclear power or the dictat of the Council of Ministers – these were NOs. The prosperous fellow was a NO; we discovered he was the owner and a local who had recently returned after living in England where he had acquired his accent and obviously made a bob or two.

In another bar at the far end of the main street we discovered that the next bus to Fermoy was not until Thursday (today was Monday) so that spoilt our plan to bus it to Fermoy and walk from there to Cork. In the light of this we figured we'd walk to Fermoy and bus from there to Cork.

A walk around town led us to the Catholic church which, according to the *Shell Guide to Ireland*, was built in the 1880s and is a Lombardo-Romanesque structure; it certainly possessed a superfluity of decoration, both inside and out, rather too much for my taste. But at least it was open. The Protestant Cathedral was firmly locked although a noticeboard declared it to be 'Open Daily for Prayer', – perhaps we were too late.

The bridge across the Blackwater is a magnificent structure. It reaches across the river from higher land on the Lismore side to a lower level on the north bank, so passes high above the water. Lismore Castle is a mass of turrets and mullioned windows set squarely in solid stone walls and rises, like a vision, out of a mass of trees. It is a sight which must have been impressing visitors for centuries. The river banks are flat grassy meadows dotted with great mature trees, some growing alone and free, with cattle grazing between, others grouped and spreading across the water.

Back in town we decided on the Lismore Hotel for our dinner. This is a very large building with a huge bar area and the potential for dealing with about a hundred times as many guests as were evident. The dining room was semi-detached from the main edifice, a high-ceilinged, octagonal-shaped room lined with maroon, striped, Regency-style wallpaper, and held a full complement of dining tables and chairs. After ordering we were entertained by the radio: the news in Gaelic and an informative programme on traditional Irish music – far preferable to BBC Radio 1.

The meal was enjoyable, though 20 years behind the times. Where Prawn Cocktail or Mushrooms in Garlic Sauce lead the starters in

England, Tomato Soup or Egg Mayonnaise still apparently rule in Ireland. My egg mayonnaise included curled cucumber slices and dessicated lettuce leaves but the sauce was sprinkled with cayenne pepper, and after the main course the friendly waitress came and asked, 'Would you like a few more chips?' - an offer we couldn't refuse! The cheese was processed, the coffee instant and the house wine pretty ghastly and hideously expensive but at the end we felt more than satisfied and were given an After Eight mint.

Lismore Castle

Lismore seemed not just quiet, but reticent, reserved, secretive, as though there was something of significance which is felt but not seen. This impression may have a connection with the town's long history. The fabric of Lismore Castle is predominantly early seventeenth and nineteenth century but it incorporates some towers from the medieval castle of the Bishops of Lismore. Prior to this was a castle built by King John and before that a monastery founded by St Carthage and a university which became a great centre of learning in the Dark Ages. The survival, indeed the flowering, of the Christian church in Ireland, after the Romans had withdrawn their civilising influence from northern Europe, is indeed remarkable. At this time there was truth in

51

the xenophobic claim that Ireland was a land of saints and scholars while England was a land of doubt and darkness. It was the incursions of the British later which converted a seat of learning here at Lismore into a fortified place.

The first Protestant bishop granted the castle to Sir Walter Raleigh who, in 1602, sold Lismore to Richard Boyle, an Elizabethan adventurer. Boyle became Earl of Cork and rebuilt the castle as his home. It fell to the Confederate Catholics in 1645; James II stayed a night in 1689 but it became neglected and largely ruinous in the following century. The castle passed by marriage to the Cavendishes and the sixth Duke of Devonshire began restoring and rebuilding when he succeeded his father in 1811. In the following year it was sufficiently habitable for him to entertain his cousin Lady Caroline Lamb, who came so that she might forget Byron. The medieval appearance of the castellated towers and turrets was added and the ruined chapel of the Bishops was restored to a ballroom of ecclesiastical character. From 1932 to 1944 the castle was continually occupied by Lord Charles Cavendish, the younger son of the ninth Duke of Devonshire and his wife, the former Miss Adele Astaire, dancer and actress (and elder sister of Fred Astaire).

We visited a couple of bars after our meal at the Lismore Hotel. The first was a young people's pub, with juke box, pool table, snooker room and fruit machines which invited clients to 'Play Video Trivia'. It occurred to me more than once that the pubs and the churches have something in common. They both have interiors which are usually colourful, much decorated, comforting enough to act as a kind of refuge from the sometimes bleak and harsh world outside.

The second bar we selected with some effort to find an ethnic shop/bar and were not disappointed. We were the only customers as we entered and found the landlord and lady behind the bar and beneath a huge television on which was showing a rugby match. The wall beyond the great bar counter revealed a mass of original fitted wooden shelving exhibiting a selection of bottles, groceries and sweets. Our man wore spectacles with lenses so thick one could scarcely see his eyes; he must have been almost blind and found his way around the bar by touch. His other half made up for his disabilities and she was very welcoming. They told us that they were the third generation of their family to run the pub and that when they passed on there would be nobody to take over; I guessed they were brother and sister.

We hardly wanted another drink but were keen to meet Irish folks.

The landlady explained that the only live music was at the weekend and that the pubs were empty in the week because people had no money. Another customer entered – a middle-aged fellow with, as we soon discovered, a marked stutter, and ordered a pint. It seemed he too was more interested in talking than drinking, for he hardly touched his Guinness. He got quite excited when we told him what we were doing – he declared that he would like to put a pack on his back and take off on foot. He swore a great deal. The landlady chided him for this and, lest we get the wrong impression, told us that he was rich and owned several businesses in the town. Our wealthy companion told us too that the Dukes of Devonshire were good landlords, and regaled us with stories about the castle and its illustrious visitors – the Mitfords and the Astaires. Sure, he had danced in the chapel-ballroom and drunk with Fred Astaire who, he told us, was the meanest man, willing to accept drinks from others but never to buy one in return.

Back at the hotel the main signs of activity were on the television screen, though the large screen above the bar carried the message, 'Only for News and Sport'; in an adjoining room was a massive flat screen television which a young lad was viewing. Television seems more ubiquitous and dominating in Ireland than it does even in England. Is this the reason why we had heard so little music, why so few people were to be found in the pubs? Ned and Eileen had eight channels from which to choose. All four UK channels were piped into the house from a powerful receiver placed on a nearby hilltop; the two Irish stations are further complemented by two satellite channels: Sky and Superchannel, both of which are pretty rubbishy. After watching BBC1 on the giant flat screen for an hour we retired.

Tuesday 25 May
After breakfast in the bar we set out to walk up-river along the Blackwater valley to cover the 15 or so miles to Fermoy. The main road on the north bank provided a much more direct link along the first leg to Ballyduff, where we would cross to the south bank to follow a minor road.

As we crossed the river from Lismore the sun burst through the overcast sky and illumined to best advantage the solid masonry bridge, the exclamation mark of a cathedral spire, the lush green meadow, the fine mature trees, the deep dark river and the large looming mass of Lismore Castle. I felt there must be a riverside path here but no sooner had we begun heading upstream than we met a creek which blocked our way. A heron standing sentinel at the point where this watercourse joined the river flapped away at our approach. We had no choice but to leave the meadow and join the road. Before doing so Tony had to be excused in the undergrowth: he had an upset stomach, perhaps an after-effect of dinner at the Lismore Hotel.

The five miles to Ballyduff were superb. The river scenery here is wonderful - wooded slopes on the north side serve as constant reminder that the country in that direction is mountainous and wild in comparison to the immediate scenes of pastoral delight. Butterflies were aflutter in the warm sunshine. And all is remarkably unpeopled, unsullied, unknown. During the two previous years my family and I had spent our summer holiday in France, mainly in the Dordogne. That is a region of hills and rivers, woods and meadows, small towns and villages. This Waterford landscape constantly reminded me of the Dordogne and I thought it odd that it was so unvisited – there were no campsites, no sign of any river-borne activity and, unfortunately, no riverside footpaths. Whilst it is true that tourism tends to destroy the very features which attracts it in the first place I felt that there was so much of this uncrowded island that was beautiful and charming that a little well regulated development would attract tourists and surely benefit the locals too.

Ballyduff is a pleasant village where we sat on a wall surrounding the churchyard to drink milk and eat chocolate. As we did so a man entered the church, presumably to say a prayer or two – the doors of the Catholic churches are ever open. The next ten miles to Fermoy passed without event or very much interest. The sun disappeared behind all-enveloping cloud and the day became dull. Tony's guts ached, he was walking slowly and developing a new crop of blisters after last week's had dried up over the weekend in Dungarvan. I must say that the tedium began to set in for me too, for the first time. Walking mile after mile along an unbroken metalled road certainly has its limitations. No matter how attractive the scenery I would always rather follow an unmade track: a green road, a field path or, in this river valley, a riverside path. Such a route is easier on the feet, affords greater variety, particularly in one's immediate surroundings, and encourages a feeling of oneness with the natural world.

Shortly out of Ballyduff our lane crossed the boundary to Cork from County Waterford. A large ornate sign bearing the county coat of arms and the gaelic inscription: *Failte so Conntae Portlairge* – Welcome to County Waterford, stood at the roadside beside a pair of finely built lime kilns. As we approached the main road a mile or two before Fermoy we had a view northwards to the Galtee Mountains and north-westwards to the rather less elevated Ballyhoura Mountains.

An old man with a stick approached us: one of those rare occasions when we met someone on the road.

'How are you, lads? he asked of us.

We told him, not entirely honestly, that we had walked from Dublin and he proceeded to give us the precise mileage to that point.

'Sure, 'tis a grand day for walking. You don't want it too hot or sunny for doing a walk.'

It was extraordinary how this old boy could expend so many words to assure us of the suitability of the weather. It was a torrent of words, all friendly and encouraging, but more or less the same few used in every possible combination and permutation to express the point. I asked if we could take a picture of him.

'Sure, you can take a photygraph of me if you so wish', and he posed with a toothy grin and one arm extended and resting with elegant poise upon his stick, a perfect portrait against a hedgebank full of cow parsley.

Cyclist in Ballyduff

'Good luck, boys, good luck.'

His parting words inspired us with fresh enthusiasm after this unexpected meeting.

We passed a sign which informed us that Fermoy is twinned with Plomeur in Brittany; one example among many which informed us that the fashion for town twinning has spread to Ireland. The main road into town was hectic with traffic, which contained a high proportion of cattle trucks and cars towing horse boxes. It was around three o'clock when we walked past the cattle market and into town, the biggest place we had encountered since leaving Dublin. The shops were busy, the pavements crowded and the roads choked almost to a standstill. Again I was reminded of France – a more prosperous country maybe, but one whose small towns exhibit a similar anarchic appearance: merchandise spills out of the shops onto the pavement, signs proliferate and properties are decorated in a dazzling variety of styles, and never one in sympathy with another but each according to the taste and inclination of its respective owner, and frequently the spaces between are simply wasted, uncared for.

The town was full of people – few tourists here but many country folk going about their essential business on this market day. Generally speaking, the Irish don't look as healthy as the English (though it has also been my observation that the English don't look as healthy as their continental counterparts) though overweight and obesity are certainly not so commonplace. Fewer people wear spectacles but more have bad teeth. Smoking, it seems, is not becoming unfashionable as it is in England; everyone in Ireland seems to indulge. There exists an extraordinary range of facial types and wide variation in hair and skin colour. They are definitely scruffier and tend to wear greens and browns - except in the cities and larger towns where folk are much more sophisticated. Flat caps remain widespread amongst the older men. They drive smaller cars which are older and more bashed.

England and Holland and Germany are more thickly populated and thus have a more established civic tradition – certainly these are countries which have been industrialised and urbanised for longer and to a greater extent than France or Ireland. Perhaps there is too, in those predominantly Protestant countries, more regimentation, less spontaneity and independence of spirit, a desire to conform, to toe the line. Yet to recall the Age of Reason and all that it achieved in France – the classical architecture and formal gardens – perhaps demolishes my argument. But was this a thin veneer through which the French

Revolution later erupted?

We queued for the bus to Cork. At least Tony and I did so while the locals simply went for it when the bus pulled in – France again. This old boneshaker was packed with secondary schoolchildren, noisy as only a bus load of kids can be, their uniforms awry, stuffing crisps and sweets for all they were worth, pushing and shoving. But there was no surreptitious smoking, nothing malicious in their behaviour and absolutely no swearing. Our bus was headed south-south-west over the hills for 20 odd miles to Cork, decanting schoolkids at various stages on the way, the last stragglers dropped only a few miles from Ireland's second city.

I'd long had a copy of Robert Gibbings' *Lovely is the Lee* but the picture he conjures was scarcely recognisable in the prospect beside the road into Cork. A lone ship was ploughing up-river past factories and warehouses, many sadly derelict. From the bus station we caught a bus to Cork Youth Hostel, a fine old house with excellent facilities and beautifully kept – a striking contrast to Arthurstown and earlier hostels. We felt it would be good to take in a theatre; I rang Cork Opera House to enquire about a play called *Sive* (rhymes with jive), by John B Keane, which the local paper said was showing 'for the third week by popular demand'; we were told there would be no problem booking a seat.

Sive is a love story and family drama of universal appeal. It is set in a rural community in the west of Ireland in the 1920s and is the tale of a young orphan girl, Sive, who lives with her embittered and scheming aunt, her kindly but ineffective uncle and her sympathetic old grandmother. Sive loves an impecunious lad from the village but her aunt wants to marry her off to some rich local farmer. The village matchmaker, a wheedling, sweet-talking hypocrite of an old man helps her in this scheme and finds a hideous but wealthy old codger who is willing to pay both matchmaker and aunt a bounty if they will persuade Sive to marry. The uncle is horrified when he discovers this plan but his protestations are smothered by the cajoling and nagging of his insufferable wife.

There are two further characters in the shape of a couple of tinkers, poor ragged fellows, one older who speaks and one younger who plays the bodhrán and sings. The tinkers are variously respected and despised by the good and bad souls respectively, but never ignored. They visit the house from time to time, begging for a morsel of food but knowing exactly what is going on in the household. The tinkers are like prophets – they understand all, accuse wrongdoers, caution them in the error of their ways and warn of impending disaster. The older tinker speaks directly to those culpable whilst the younger tinker, like a calypso singer, but with a presence and profundity which cannot be ignored, sets his thoughts to verse and sings them to the accompaniment of his thumping bodhrán. The matchmaker is cursed, ulterior motives are exposed; all those with evil intent are faced with the truth and issued a warning.

Do people like those tinkers still exist in Ireland? They are psychologists, social workers, prophets, poets and musicians in one compelling package – there is something of a medieval nature about them.

As the play develops one inevitably sympathises with Sive and hopes desperately that she and her boyfriend will win through in the end. The heroes and villains are obvious but the final outcome is not. In case the reader is not acquainted with the final denouement, I will not give it away her. Suffice it to say that to me it was totally unexpected, a complete shock which, on reflection, seemed a very Irish conclusion. It is a powerful drama, deeply involving and not without humour and, on this weekday evening in Cork Opera House, faultlessly performed. I have since learnt that when Sive was first staged by the Cork-based Southern Theatre Group in the late 1950s it was scorned by the Abbey Theatre in Dublin which would have nothing to do with it. There are a host of stories about John B Keane, the writer who owns a pub in Listowel, County Kerry, a town which plays host to an annual literary festival.

As we left the hostel for the theatre we met up with a friend of mine from home, Brian Richards, who was on holiday in Ireland. The three of us had seen the play and now we hurried through a shower of rain into a pub. Tony was on lemonade so as not to offend his upset guts. We discussed the play; eventually Tony emerged from a deep silence, turned to us and declared, 'That was a bloody good play.' Now I was sure he had enjoyed it I felt this had somehow compensated for a less than wonderful day's walking.

Brian told us that there was a festival being held over the approaching weekend at Kenmare, County Kerry. This event promised plenty of music. Tony and I decided then to spend the weekend in Kenmare. The projected three days' walking from Cork to Killarney appeared, on the evidence of the map, not to be terribly exciting, except the last third through Kerry where the landscape becomes more mountainous. We now planned to take the train to Killarney the next day, and aimed to finish our walk after three days from Killarney to some point on the Atlantic coast, probably Waterville, where we would return to Kenmare via the Ring of Kerry.

Wednesday 26 May
We spent an inadequate hour or two walking around Cork before catching that train. Cork is a large, bustling city. There are some fine buildings but quite a bit of tattiness too. The people in the streets seem on the whole smarter, more sophisticated and wear clothes of lighter shades than those in the country towns we'd visited. Beggars abound, often children; one small boy of about ten years was singing for all his worth, a barefoot young girl proffered a can, an inebriated, red-faced man held out his hand beside a church. A small green contained benches where I noticed several people reading Bibles; on another patch of grass a memorial to the victims of Hiroshima and Nagasaki bore the message, 'That it may never happen again'.

The railway leaves Cork and heads north via Blarney to reach Mallow on the River Blackwater, then follows the Blackwater upstream due west to Rathmore, just across the border in Kerry. To the south the Boggeragh Mountains merge into the Derrynasaggert Mountains, the latter partly in Kerry. Here the landscape becomes more interesting. Further peaks, often curiously isolated and therefore more impressive, rise out of the undulating countryside. A pair of near identical hills, which the most pure-minded and unimaginative could not help but liken to a pair of female breasts, appear to the south. This likeness is further emphasised by the summit cairns which give the appearance of nipples on the breasts. These are The Paps, 2,273 and 2,284 feet apiece. In Irish folklore, they represent the breasts of Anu or Danu, the Celtic goddess of plenty, responsible for the fertility of Munster.

Killarney is the centre of a tourist industry which has been thriving here since British tourism was invented, that is since Georgian times, when for the first time people sought the scenery of mountains and lakes. Prior to this, mountains were regarded with dread, as places to be avoided, where evil spirits dwelt and the mind and hand of man made no impression. The cult of the picturesque, as defined by William Gilpin, and the love of wild and natural landscape so enthusiastically expressed by Wordsworth and his followers, fuelled the Romantic Age, the inevitable reaction to the supremacy of reason, of industry and of man's dominion over Nature.

Yet perhaps because Ireland never underwent an Industrial Revolution, because the Irish psyche was never moulded by a reaction to the Age of Industry which laid the foundation of the Romantic Movement, Irish mountains remain largely unappreciated and unused. There is no tradition of hill walking and mountain climbing as there is in England, Scotland and Wales, as evidenced by the fact that there are no paths over the hills, no summit cairns (except the Paps) and no people, a point made by Richard Mersey in his recent book *The Hills of Cork and Kerry* (Gill and Macmillan/Alan Sutton, 1987). This is a splendid book by one who, although he has walked in far more exotic locations, including the Himalayas, writes eloquently in praise of the mountains of Munster. His prose is absolutely convincing, and especially so when contrasted with certain of his comments of a more negative nature: 'I detest the Gap of Dunloe and all it contains. It is part of the truly awful tourism of Killarney.'

The Kerry mountains are recognised as a tourist attraction but only insomuch as they form a backdrop to Killarney and the lakes, not as an attraction in themselves. If Killarney were in the English Lake District it would boast several shops selling outdoor gear and climbing equipment, and the pubs would contain their complement of booted and bearded adventurers discussing the next day's expedition.

The reality is different, however. Killarney is certainly full of shops, and bars and restaurants, but the shops sell every conceivable knick-knack and souvenir (and some inconceivable until you see them with your own eyes). At the station we were beseiged with offers of B & B, hotel accommodation, taxis to our destination and by guys touting for Killarney Youth Hostel and an independent hostel which was 25 pence cheaper. Both had a minibus, with suitable livery, to provide the weary traveller with a free lift.

After partaking of tea and sandwiches in a bar full of Americans we set out. At last we found a Protestant church with an open door and took the opportunity to view. It was certainly reminiscent of any English parish church with its memorials to former rectors, parishioners fallen in battle or simply passed on. In addition the interior contained some elaborate and perfectly applied stencilling around its walls. I remained unmoved by the building as a whole.

We checked a large map outside the Tourist Information Office and found the pleasant way out of town, by a path beside the lake. After a few minutes and a slight rise we discovered the scene transformed. The crowds and commercial excess of Killarney had given way to wonderful, inspiring vistas across the wide, flat, calm waters of Lough Leane to the wooded slopes and naked mountains beyond. It was a sunny and spacious afternoon and the whole panorama of peaks was visible. The highest mountains lay to the south-west. Carrauntoohil, Ireland's highest peak at 3,414 feet, stood out among the clustering summits of the range known as Macgillycuddy's Reeks, a name which always puts me in mind of an old man's stinking socks.

Following the path and lake shore as far as a creek and large hotel, we were forced to retreat to the main road. Here we found an interesting church, a contemporary structure whose plan is a regular octagon. The side opposite the entrance is a sheet of glass so that the view from the pews and beyond the altar is to the mountains. In the foreground, but outside, stands a large plain wooden cross. This place of worship is known as the Church of Peace and Reconciliation, an apt dedication for these times in Ireland.

Since arriving in Ireland some nine days before I'd had a distant but persistent awareness that I was walking across a small island, a part of which was torn by communal strife, though there was practically no sign of such in this southern half of the island. From here it seemed a pointless waste, crazy but tragic. Ireland has other problems: underdevelopment, unemployment, economic uncertainty, emigration. Finding a solution for these is surely hampered by the troubles in the North. The troubles don't stop at the border, though, as I have said, there are few visible signs of them this far south. Tourism is surely affected – Ireland should be a popular destination, with the present boom in holidays based upon some outdoor activity. I put this point to a young Irish fellow later that day but he accused me of a blackmailing approach – solve the troubles to reap an economic reward.

The opposing views of the two communities in Northern Ireland seem irreconcilable but there must be a mutual benefit to be gained in ending the strife and establishing a peaceful regime, and there is surely more to that than the withdrawal of British troops. I was beginning to appreciate Irish nationalism (though I've always been repelled by any form of English nationalism) and the feelings engendered by a long history of struggle for independence by the Irish from their British overlords. I'd really had little idea how different the Irish were, how much like a recently established, ex-colonial nation Ireland was, and how far the experience of history shapes the character and attitudes of a people.

We planned to walk via the north bank and north-west corner of the lake and then to ascend the Gap of Dunloe which pierces the mountains to reach Black Valley Youth Hostel, a distance of about 12 miles. The road began to climb as we approached Kate Kearney's Cottage, about half-way. This so-called cottage is a mini-complex containing a shop and a great barn-like bar where we fortified ourselves with a pint of Guinness (Tony was back on the booze) before tackling the Gap. It was quite late on; the jaunting cars (horse-drawn buggies) had stopped running. The horses were variously tethered or roaming loose outside while a number of the drivers, or 'jarvies', were sat round a table, already well cut, and enjoying a game of cards from which they derived endless merriment.

Approaching the Gap of Dunloe

The sky was broken but clouds clung to the high mountains each side of the valley as we climbed the stony track. One stray jaunting car passed us on its return to Kate Kearney's. The way rose gradually but not consistently through the gap, past several small lakes. The continued lack of rain was evident in the dried up stream beds hereabouts. Derelict cottages provided a stark contrast to the modern bungalows we'd passed on the low road west of Killarney, which in this favoured position seemed plusher and more sophisticated than elsewhere.

The overwhelming feature of the scene is rock: chippings underfoot, boulders and bedrock at one's side and in the stream beds, and great sawn-off sections lining the steep walls of the valley. And rock unseen, an endless mass, forming the soaring peaks at every hand. To our left rose Purple Mountain, though the convex summit was out of sight; to our right, the mighty Reeks. The rock here is Old Red Sandstone, a compact and massive stone of certain reddish hue, smooth and rounded from a distance but rough and tough as coarse sandpaper to the touch. When seen in cross-section the strata are greatly contorted. Some variety is provided by the intrusion of veins of white quartz or milkstone.

The silence was all pervasive, there were no streams to gurgle, the windless evening left the lakes unruffled, there were no rustling trees, only inert rock, still water and somnolent mountains. We eventually reached the head of the Gap, at 795 feet, and from there gained a breathtaking view down Black Valley, and onward to mountains in every direction. The track took a long way round by a hairpin bend to reach the hostel which we could pick out beside a church below. We stepped over a barbed wire fence and scrambled down a tussocky hillside.

The youth hostel was occupied by a large number of Irish teenagers, noisy but harmless, and a smattering of American, Canadian and Australian travellers, mainly cyclists. We'd bought some vegetables and meat in Killarney in order to cook a stew at the hostel.

Thursday 27 May
The next morning we examined the cupboards to see if any food had been left. I found a packet of sunflower seeds and was halfway through eating them when an English guy claimed them as his own. He proceeded to make a breakfast mixture from raw oats and Ribena and on these he sprinkled the remaining sunflower seeds. We guessed he was a vegan; he told us he worked part-time - some sort of social worker we understood – and thought everybody else should too. From other remarks we also surmised he was divorced, or separated, and appeared an unhappy person. He seemed to lack an essential energy

and I wondered whether this was due to his veganism.

I'd acquired a one inch to one mile map of the Killarney District and it was a relief to see exactly where we were headed. From Black Valley Youth Hostel the road heads south-eastwards to cross the Gearhameen River which drains the Reeks and flows into the Killarney lakes a mile or two further east. Our planned route followed the road between the mountains and through gaps, first south, then west, then south, then west again. By then we should be out of the mountains and heading down to Sneem, more or less at sea-level, about 20 miles from Dunloe Gap by this route.

For sheer walking pleasure, this day was the best. The weather was ideal: mainly sunshiny, with a gentle breeze blowing at us from the west, now warming, now cooling. The first mile or two, around the 100 feet contour, was through a jumbled country of rocks and yellow-flowering gorse and lush grass which was completely natural but in which these simple elements were so perfectly arranged that one almost suspected the hand of some artful designer. Now we began a steady climb up the valley of the River Owenreagh, at first passing a series of delightful miniature waterfalls and the occasional farmhouse or cottage with characteristic garish paintwork: lilac or torquoise or puce.

The countryside became wilder with increased altitude until we arrived at the head of the valley where we enjoyed tremendous views in all directions. Directly ahead is the sharp, distinctive peak of Mullaghanattin, known as the 'Matterhorn of Ireland'. Before it lies Lough Brin, overseen by a solitary farmhouse at the foot of a great slope which sweeps uncompromisingly skyward through 1,700 feet in well under a mile.

Now we followed the road south by a valley which carried the River Lealduff; here the mountains were not as closely clustered and the countryside became more open and spacious. At a crossroads we asked an old man on a bicycle if there was a bar in the vicinity and were told that there was one a couple of hundred metres straight ahead. We were surprised to be answered in metres. We walked on maybe 500 metres but without sight of a bar. Perhaps our guide meant a couple of kilometres; however, we turned back disappointed to resume our route. It was mid-afternoon as a number of coaches passed us, some with English licence plates, all evidently heading back to Killarney after an afternoon's tour of the Ring of Kerry. Eventually we caught sight of the Kenmare River, so called, although this long inlet of the Atlantic is really a drowned valley. Here I rejoiced at the sight of

In the Reeks – Mullaghanattin in the distance

fuschia hedges, the first we'd seen, the blood red droplets still mainly in bud, though a number had opened.

Sneem we thought sounded like a toothpaste or a furniture polish. It is in fact a sizeable village which is arranged in two distinct halves, each with its own village green, one north of the river and one south. In each case the rows of houses focus on their respective greens. At first glance it all looks rather English but on closer inspection the essential Irishness of the place is evident, most obviously in the rampant individualism of the colours used to paint the outsides of cottages. But Sneem remains an attractive settlement on the tourist-frequented Ring of Kerry. The impact of tourism has made itself felt: there are a number of restaurants and rather plush Lounge Bars. We had our first pint in one owned by an American, then chose a restaurant which turned out to be run by a Dutch family. The food was OK but bland and lacking the sort of bulk you need after a 20 mile walk. When we left the restaurant we set out to find a bar unaffected by tourism.

We found one at a corner of the village. The interior was gloomy, the walls painted in the bright blue of swimming pools though somewhat darkened by the fumes of tobacco and Guinness and quite bare save for an out of date calendar. I asked the old man behind the bar for a couple of pints. He seemed a bit put out at this request, took two dirty glasses from the stack on the counter, sloshed them under a cold water tap and proceeded to fill them. Pouring Guinness is no rapid business but this old codger took an absolute age. His eyes were almost shut and he appeared not to be able to see very well. And he was terrible slow: in fact to observe his movements was like watching a film in slow motion. It seemed he could only just raise his hand to the top of the handle to pull a pint. When they were eventually ready I felt awful about giving him a £20 note - we had no smaller between us. He took another age to count out the change and when he'd done so I found that he'd considerably undercharged us.

The Guinness was pretty bad, it was flat and tasted very old – perhaps the prices he charged matched the age of the brew. Two other fellows were drinking. They were maybe in their fifties, one jacketed and sitting on a stool, the other raincoated and standing, and both drinking with some determination. The occasional demands of these two customers kept the old man flat out. The television was on; no one spoke. The gloom intensified almost to the point of invisibility. Tony and I were sat beneath the window and could make out larger shapes in the dying remnants of daylight. One of the drinkers approached the window to sort out the money from his trouser pocket. He smiled at us but said nothing. No one suggested switching on a light. Tony left his stout and we retreated into one of the plush lounge bars where the television also ruled. When I first visited Ireland in 1970 I don't remember seeing any TVs in bars and was delighted so easily to fall into amusing, stimulating conversation with intelligent folk. Things seem to have changed for the worse in this respect.

We returned to our Tourist Board approved bungalow B & B and sat in the living room for a spell. There was a piano. Tony sought permission to tickle the ivories although the instrument was desperately out of tune. The teenage daughter of the house soon joined in on the guitar but the crack came to an abrupt end when mother called daughter away. It was fairly late and there were other guests. We tactfully retired.

Friday 28 May

After breakfast with two couples – one American and the other German – we set out for our last day's walk. The Killarney District Map stops just short of Sneem and my only reference was the quarter inch map of Cork and Kerry. This showed a minor road or track heading west for three or four miles reverting into something less distinct (the line on the map becomes dotted), up to a gap and then into a road again beside the extensive Lough Currane and eventually to Waterville and Ballinskelligs Bay. This point would give us an unimpaired view over the Atlantic Ocean where we would feel our trans-Ireland walk, albeit with considerable omissions, had been accomplished.

'The clouds sat low on the hills'

It had rained in the night and, although the rain was over, the day was damp and misty and the clouds sat very low on the hills, to obscure all but the lowest slopes. We crossed the bridge connecting the two halves of Sneem (I wondered if there is rivalry and a name for Sneemians depending upon which bank they live) and looked down onto the river bed, naked Old Red Sandstone, the river a mere trickle. We found the minor road which I guessed had formerly been the route west and now ran parallel with the main road. The lane bore right into

67

a forest at a point where a broken down bridge was signposted as Dangerous. We eventually descended to a river bed and scrambled up the far side to continue by the track. We crossed a peat bog and then reached a farm at a point near the main road.

The way from here was not at all evident and we asked a man herding cows. Perhaps his reply was in Gaelic but to us it was incomprehensible. I realised we had to head uphill rather to the north of a gap. We found a break in the thick forest and struggled up a squelching morass. It was like walking through deep treacle; at the top we were drenched from the knees down. From a high point nearby we could see the Kenmare River; on our right was a mountainside reaching up into the clouds. Tony wasn't happy. I knew we should be on the far side of that mountain heading west. We asked an old man bottle-feeding a goat but he seemed not to know what was on the far side. We carried on over difficult ground on the flank of the mountain, within sight of the Kenmare River, all the time looking out for signs of a track over the top and sometimes trekking through cloud and out of sight. I felt determined to find Lough Currane and reach Waterville but loth to tackle an unknown mountainside without a map.

Emerging from the cloud on a bluff I could see a watery shore in the distance and told myself it was the lough, but it was still the Kenmare River! I felt cheated myself as we performed our last cheat and descended the hillsides and lanes towards Castle Cove. In fact this was very nearly the open sea and no doubt the Atlantic Ocean made its presence felt hereabouts. We found a hotel and had a drink and a sandwich in the bar. The barmaid seemed very defensive in answering Tony's remark that it must be quiet out of season. The one other fellow at the bar was mouthing words at us but uttering no sound. I thought he was codding us until the barmaid explained that he was deaf and dumb. Perhaps that was why she'd taken umbrage at our remark about it being quiet here.

Our silent companion communicated by his animated expressions and by passing us notes on scraps of paper. We discovered there were no buses and no other means of reaching Kenmare, a good 25 miles distant. There was nothing for it but to hitch a lift. This we tried for over an hour. It was then we fully appreciated how little traffic there is on Irish roads. Eventually a German registered Land Rover pulled up. Its two Teutonic occupants offered us a lift to Kenmare to which they were heading. We'd walked about nine miles although it felt much further and we gratefully piled in. The woman driving was an agricultural student at Dublin and her friend, a gentle pigtailed guy, was on holiday. They appeared to be discussing the landscape with some excitement; at one point the woman pulled up, jumped out, picked some wild mint, returned with it and we all sampled that wild sweet smell of the bog.

Kenmare is a fair-sized town: it is full of shops and bars, the legacy of serving a large chunk of West Kerry, the Inveragh and Beara Peninsulas, much of the hinterland and settlements beside the Roughty valley to the east. We found an excellent room in the attic of a hotel-bar in the main street. The town was buzzing. The main street was lined with cars and the 'square' in front of the town green was filling up with stalls. These offered for sale anything and everything from fast food – fish and chips, burgers, or alternative food such as chilli beans in pitta bread – and all manner of merchandise from hand-thrown pots and jars of goat's cheese to cheap plastic knick-knackery. We wandered around enjoying the activity, and I found the people to be of the greatest interest.

We found a seat in a crowded bar. Many of the drinkers were locals – country folk judging by their red faces and rough clothes, and many were from overseas: Germans, Dutch, English. These people were not tourists but obviously lived here. Their age and appearance suggested they might have been at home at a 1960s open air pop concert or present day CND demo. Their children were attractive but small versions of their parents in their cut-down kaftans and patched jeans. There was no segregation here and this unexpected mixture seemed perfectly normal.

A pair of musicians struck up in one corner: a middle-aged man on fiddle and a young woman on pipes (father and daughter?). Passers by flocked in and it was soon standing room only. I was sitting beside the door, my eyes gazing at a disembodied hand clutching a miniature cassette recorder thrust into the room to record this rendering of traditional Irish music. This part of Ireland has a way of life and a culture which is probably among the most traditional and unchanged in Europe. This attracts numbers of youngish people, 'the Sixties Generation', from the most 'advanced' nations to put down roots in Cork and Kerry. Cottages are cheap and land is even cheaper, which all helps them attempt a self-sufficient lifestyle. In order to raise the small amount of cash they need, I guess they trade their wares at events such as the Kenmare Festival.

The festival itself was billed as a *Cibeal*, a Gaelic word, the theme of which was the Sweeney, to which there were references everywhere. A handbill listed the weekend's events, and copies of these were posted up in the windows of the town's shops and bars. A series of lectures was being held in one bar. These included astrology and self-hypnosis, hardly traditional Irish culture, or was it? Certainly one or two Irish females whom I've known in the past have taken a great interest in such matters.

Of the main activity of the *Cibeal* – drinking – nothing was said. I have never seen so much booze consumed by so many people over such a long period. We arrived on Friday evening and left on Sunday afternoon. Every time we left the hotel there were crowds of people drinking in the streets, outside the bars, of which there was a great number. Saturday was sunny and hot so the carefree atmosphere was emphasised. On the Friday we went to a concert – a one-man show (plus sound engineer) – in one of the bars. The singer was small, intense, much practised, a virtuoso performer, a perfectionist in his craft. He wrote all his own material and one had to admit he was good but after it I felt rather unmoved.

Saturday 29 May

The next morning we ambled, in the warm sunshine, down to the quay. Kenmare lies close at the head of the Kenmare River and is the first crossing point. From the quay we gazed west-south-west across the sea-salt water to the ocean, some 30 miles distant. Back in town we found the lecturing pub and waited for the back room to clear for a lecture on trees. The talk was given by an Englishman, fortyish, a working forester who had been living and working in Cork for the past 15 years. He sat smoking roll-ups and supping bottled Guinness. He knew his trees intimately. He explained that Ireland had once been covered in trees but that some climatic and climactic change in medieval times had wiped out the forest cover. It is commonly held that the British robbed Ireland of its trees, – it is true that many British ships were built of Irish oaks – but the denudation of Ireland was more an Act of God than an Act of the Brits.

Our lecturer explained that conditions today – the constant rainfall, the wet ground, the absence of frost and general lack of extremes of weather – were ideal for tree growing. We were told that conifers grew three times as fast here as in Sweden. I could vouch for the tree growing potential of Ireland's otherwise difficult landscape: on our walk through the mountains to Sneem I'd noticed that split stakes used as fence posts to which barbed wire was nailed had taken root and were actually sprouting leaves. In recent years the Irish government has been pursuing a policy of afforestation, the total land devoted to forestry doubling in the past ten years, though two thirds of this is Sitka spruce and most of the rest dominated by one or two other species. However, some five per cent of the newly forested land is devoted to broad-leaved trees (half of it birch) compared to less than one per cent in Wales.

The tree-enthusiast opened and closed his session with a poem. He certainly loved his trees; he spoke about individual ones he knew like old friends. But he was impatient with the Irish authorities for concentrating their efforts on so few species and so lacking imagination, aesthetic sense and practical wisdom (monoculture leaves species prone to disease). He could list 150 species which he reckoned would grow well in Ireland. He would have liked to cover the land with trees, well-spaced so that animals could graze the grass between but close enough that you could 'lose the people'. Here, one felt, was a man with a vision: a vision of a varied and enriched landscape centred on his beloved trees - this would be the making of Ireland – a land which would sustain a prospering people. We spent a fascinating and enjoyable hour in his company.

An art exhibition in a local hall offered endless variations on the image of the image of Sweeney, half-man/half-bird, the persecuted outcast who provided the theme for this weekend's binge, sorry – *Cibeal*. There has been a recent revival of interest in the story of Sweeney though he doesn't seem to figure in many collections of Irish folklore. The modern fame of Sweeney dates back to an Irish/English edition published in 1913, then to many writers since who have employed the character in their work and most significantly to Seamus Heaney's new translation *Sweeney Astray*, published in the early 1980s. It is surely Sweeney as outsider, as a kind of weird, harassed, ever-seeking anti-hero which appeals today.

The story of Sweeney is featured in medieval texts but the character has his origins in a local Irish king who led his men in the Battle of Moira (AD 637). Prior to this Sweeney, in a fit of rage, had attacked the Christian missionary Ronan and thrown his psalter into a lake. Although the psalter is miraculously returned undamaged by an otter, Ronan, in a rather pre-Christian manner, lays a curse on Sweeney -

He shall roam Ireland, mad and bare
He shall find death on the point of a spear

71

Sweeney is now Sweeney astray, a bird flitting from tree to tree, from peak to peak, living on watercress. shivering in cruel winds, and expressing his guilt and his longing for rest in startling verse.

The text of *Sweeney Astray* is full of references to the topography and natural history of Ireland and Western Scotland. There is a beautiful rhapsody in which Sweeney praises the trees and wild flowers of Ireland – the oak, the hazel, the alder, the blackthorn, the apple, the briar, the yew, the holly, the ash, the birch, the aspen, and then the flowers. The delight in the variety and characteristics of so many species reminds one of the pastoral tradition of English poetry, but of a much later age.

One begins to feel quite sorry for the haunted Sweeney – will he ever find release? Eventually Sweeney begins to accept responsibility for his excruciating predicament – 'I have deserved all this', though he seems even more tormented as a result. He eventually meets a holy man, Moling, who takes pity on him and offers him food, though Sweeney accepts that his fate will now be violent death. Moling however promises him a Christian burial and in the meantime permits him to fly off every day on condition that he returns each evening, when he feeds on a meal of milk left him by Moling's cook. A woman suggests to the cook's husband, a swineherd, that his wife fancies Sweeney (though in fact a bird, Sweeney is perceived by humans as a man), the husband sees red and slays the unfortunate creature with a spear.

On his deathbed Sweeney repents, makes a confession to Moling and receives the last rites. So Ronan's curse is fulfilled, there's no solace for Sweeney in this life but through repentance and with the aid of a priest he finds peace and, we are assured, 'his spirit fled to heaven', as he wished. Afterwards Moling and his followers remembered Sweeney and every place alighted with reverence.

After the startling images of Mad Sweeney we returned to the pub where we'd been drawn by the promise of a poetry reading. We were waiting, in vain, for an astrologer to finish her session when only one poet out of three scheduled to take part showed up. He eventually left in disgust, a victim of the greater interest in the occult and his fellow artists' dilatoriness.

In the evening we made our way to a local hotel with an enormous hall where the band Patrick Street were to play. Due to begin at 10.30pm, the main attraction eventually showed just after midnight and continued until well past two in the morning. The bar ran the entire length of one side of the hall and was in a constant state of siege so that by the time Patrick Street arrived most people had had a skinful and, apart from a fairly serious group sitting in rows in the centre of the hall, the bulk of the 'audience' were standing in noisy confusion downing booze for all they were worth. Most people, it seemed, would have been as content with a skiffle group as with one of Ireland's leading bands. Patrick Street played a wonderful mixture of traditional and modern music on fiddle, accordion, guitar and mandoline. There were appeals from the musicians that people should shut up and listen but most people continued to ignore the music and to 'drink your faces off' as your man on stage so picturesquely put it. With an entrance fee of £5 per head and the huge amount of booze consumed during the evening the turnover must have run into several thousand pounds.

This night was the finale, fitting or otherwise, to our Irish jaunt, the peak of the almighty binge that was the Kenmare *Cibeal*. In truth, the majority of those present were Irish youngsters, sleeping in broken tents, scrapping with each other, chasing the opposite sex, blowing what little money they had getting drunk, in short acting like normal youngsters anywhere. But where was the spirit of Mad Sweeney?

Sunday 30 May
The brilliant sunshine and social abandon of that Saturday in Kenmare contrasted with Sunday's overcast sky and atmosphere of anti-climax. I opened a window on the hotel's first floor and gazed up and down the street outside - folk were still drinking at 9 o'clock in the morning, but gone was the *joie de vivre* of the day before.

Our Irish jaunt was over. There was no more walking, the long spell of fine weather was breaking, the train ride to Dublin was followed by a period of killing time before our flight home and a reunion with our families. Once we headed back east the feeling of homesickness set in. On the walk from Heuston Station to Mountjoy Square I saw Dublin through those jaundiced eyes – the Liffey, a malodorous river full of junk, often hideous modern buildings quite out of sympathy with those of a past age, the latter sometimes derelict and burnt out, the only building not in need of a coat of paint the Virgin Megastore, the shops and offices fortified with shutters and grilles, the gaps between plastered with advertisements for booze, political parties and warnings to hard drug users of the dangers of contracting AIDS by sharing needles.

Monday 1 June
Monday was Bank Holiday and everything was shut, except the pubs. Without a guide to direct us to the more attractive parts of the city we wandered aimlessly but managed to take in some of those wonderful Georgian streets and squares for which Dublin is justly famous. We wanted to take in a play so, naturally, visited the Abbey Theatre. There we saw a new play, *Say Cheese!*, by Bernard Farrell. The catchphrase referred to a farce dealing with marriage and the recent Irish phenomenon of the Wedding Fair during which, for a few days, a hotel acts as host to all the local businesses which have an interest in the wedding industry – everything from the wedding breakfast to the video of the whole event, something which can cost the happy couple dearly. The play was meant to be funny and people were laughing but I guess it was also meant to be a satire on the excesses of modern matrimony and, by implication, the drift of Irish society away from traditional values to those of a more materialistic, exploitative age. The ending was happy (but truthful?) and much of the laughter was evoked by the thwarted pretensions of the upwardly mobile middle-aged heroine. One felt that many in the audience identified with her yearnings and the laughter acted as a release to their own feelings of insecurity.

Say Cheese! was as disappointing as John B Keane's *Sive* was unexpectedly brilliant. In the theatre foyer afterwards I found and bought a copy of Keane's first novel *The Bodhrán Makers* which I subsequently read. Set in the West of Ireland in the 1950s, a period of rapid depopulation, the folk drawn mainly to the factories and building sites of England – the reader becomes acquainted with a whole cast of characters from a small country town and an outlying village.

The author relates a conflict between the members of these respective communities: the more sophisticated town dwellers look down and disapprove of their easy-going country cousins who are happy with traditional ways. The villain of the piece is the parish priest, an unbending firebrand of a man who sets out to use his undoubted power in a mission to 'civilise' the wayward villagers, in particular, to cure their penchant for boozy dances and musical sessions. He views the bodhrán – a primitive drum fashioned from wood and goatskin – as the epitome of all that is unchristian and to be suppressed. The heroes are the bodhrán player, the bodhrán maker, and their respective wives. The village schoolteacher, a boozer and philanderer, but a good man and a loved teacher, is the reluctant intermediary between the two communities.

The characterisation and dialogue ring true; the author is tender towards his characters but never sentimental or one-sided, though he is especially sympathetic towards the impoverished villagers who wrest a meagre and precarious living by digging turf and keeping a few cows.

One inevitably takes sides and hopes that the villagers, with their music and dancing – for it is their full-blooded participation in these occasional binges which keeps them sane and makes life bearable – will win the day. But as the story unfolds we begin to see the sourpuss parish priest, his snooping, gossiping housekeeper and the smug shopkeepers in the town coming out on top.

As in *Sive* the reader is encouraged to choose a side – and there is surely no question as to which – but, as in *Sive*, there is a surprise ending. In *The Bodhrán Makers* it is the heroes' emigration. One is happy in the knowledge that the exiled villagers will join friends and relations in England but one is sad that the traditional way of life will vanish. After striking against the priest by refusing to attend mass at his church the heroes admit that one compensation of emigrating will be to attend Mass once again but also to leave behind the tyranny of the priest and the institutional church and the humbug and hypocrisy of certain prevalent social attitudes. Yet, above all this, they will be relieved to escape the hard life of unremitting toil on the land. Emigration is a partial defeat but at least it offers hope for the future - for the individual leaving, but for the nation left behind .... ?

If I had discovered Ireland in these past two weeks surely Tony had rediscovered the country of his forebears and this seemed to have been a revelation. As we left to return to England I was more than ever attracted by this island on the periphery of Europe, saddened by some aspects of its 'modernisation' but inspired by its beauty and enduring difference and fascinated more than enough to know I shall return.

According to Anderson

When you walk, as distinct from drive, through a landscape, you are on equal terms with it unless, like me, you are seriously under-prepared for the bodily wear and tear it entails. There is a spiritual, as well as physical element in walking and, like the most rewarding human activities, it renders the two in harmony.

I was conscious of none of this when Roger Jones invited me to share his Irish walk. I think my ready acceptance surprised both of us. He had already conquered London to Land's End in what is my favourite of his books on walking in his beloved West of England. Apart from my family connection with Ireland, there was no obvious reason for me to embark on such a rigorous enterprise.

My previous visits had all been in a family context: as a child sharing my parents' holidays or, latterly, as husband and father. Roger knew most of the characters who linked me with Ireland. His presence and inspiration proved decisive.

So, the jaunt according to Anderson takes the shape of an outpouring of what that remarkable, sad country induces in me after forty-odd years of close connection. I thank God for a kind of healing, which Roger's almost casual suggestion has wrought.

My father left Ireland in 1936, at the age of 17, to seek work in England. He died in 1964, aged 46. I thought a great deal about him as we walked through Ireland. I have attempted here to recreate his experience from what I know of his life and have woven together this story with the account of my own journey in 1987. In the following pages my father's story is distinguished by being set in italics.

Tony Anderson
Addlestone
Surrey
January 1989

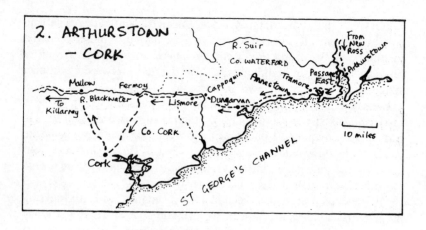

2. ARTHURSTOWN – CORK

R. Suir
Co. WATERFORD
From New Ross
Arthurstown
Mallow   Fermoy
R. Blackwater
To Killarney
Lismore
Cappoquin   Annestown
Dungarvan
Tramore
Passage East
Co. CORK
Cork
ST GEORGE'S CHANNEL
10 miles

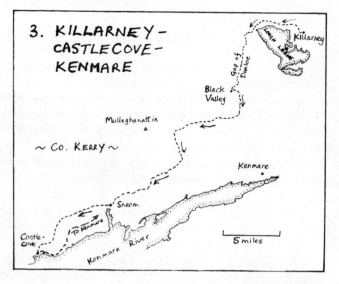

3. KILLARNEY – CASTLECOVE – KENMARE

Killarney
Gap of Dunloe
Black Valley
Mullaghanattin
~ CO. KERRY ~
Kenmare
Sneem
To Kenmare
Castle-Cove
Kenmare River
5 miles

1936

The crossing was awful. The Waterford to Fishguard boat was too small and as the waves sent it up, over and down, so went his stomach. 'Oh God, why am I here?' Around him men were drunk on Guinness, being sick over the rail, singing incomprehensible songs about the Emerald Isle. He suddenly knew that paralysis in his guts that grips when you just don't care any more. He thought of his mother, diminutive, devout, weeping endlessly all through the 24 hours before his departure. Everyone wept eventually. Tom Britt, his best friend, couldn't stop.

'Good luck, Tony,' he'd blubbered.

His father had summoned the assistance of various saints, Jesus, Mary and Joseph; and his sisters felt obliged to join their mother's wails.

At Fishguard Harbour, the wind was an icy knife. He shivered through the night-time air into the maroon and gold Great Western Railway carriage. He put the brown paper parcel, containing his worldly possessions, on the rack and sat back, exhausted, closed his eyes and pictured Kate. Six months previously, his father had forbidden him to see Kate. It had hardened his resolve. Through the summer, he'd taken her to Helvick and Ring, Clonea and Cappoquin. He was good at keeping secrets was Tony Anderson, bad at hiding his feelings. To him, she was just like Sive, John B Keane's innocent, tragic heroine.

1987

'How are your feet, Tone?' asked Roger, as we left Cork Opera House.

'I almost forgot the pain,' I replied. The play Sive which we had just seen had captured both of us. We'd walked over one hundred miles to Cork and my feet provided ample evidence of my ill-preparation.

'I've just thought of something', I ventured.

'What?' asked my old friend.

'My Dad must have been part of this: tinkers, matchmakers and farmers, he was just a country boy, really.'

Outside Cork's *An Oige* (Youth Hostel), we'd met Brian Richards, a lover of Ireland and member of the same peace group in England as Roger. We were guided to a bar, where we discussed, at length, the depths of Irish superstition. Somehow, I knew my Dad was not quite exempt from this and, in spite of reason, neither was I.

In Keane's play, humour is used cleverly to lull you into believing that the young girl is faced with the option of marrying the old farmer, whom she loathes, unless the boy who loves her can get away. Of course, the other characters (save her old grandmother) conspire to convince Sive of Liam's indifference. So the climax develops gently and then gathers pace. Unexpectedly, she runs away into the bog and is drowned. The effect is shatteringly brilliant. Outside the bar, it was pouring with rain. Keeping up with Roger and Brian was hard. I lagged behind, feeling distinctly homesick. The following morning, we took the train from Cork to Killarney.

Tony carried his brown paper parcel awkwardly down the platform at Staines West, wishing he were back in Abbeyside playing pitch and toss with Tom or sitting by the old ruined castle at Clonea with Kate.

'Tony', said a very Irish voice.

'Aunt Bess?'

Aunt Bess was his father's sister, who had married a Somerset soldier. He was often away campaigning, but had started a general provisions business in Egham. Behind the barrier he saw two teenage girls and a little boy. On the road outside was a Model T Ford, a black 'Tin Lizzie'. At the wheel sat Mell, the oldest of three sisters. When she released him from a matronly hug the like of which he'd not experienced before (Tony's mother, Hannah, was small and delicate), Aunt Bess began the formalities.

'Welcome to England, young man. Let me introduce you to your cousins Vera and Bess; and this is little Paddy.'

He was later to learn that Bess was known as 'Petsy', because she was the pet, and Vera was 'Dumpsy' - a legacy of her childhood inability to manage better than 'Humpsy Dumpsy sat on a wall.' He immediately found her large brown eyes irresistible. In the car, he met Mell, who talked as she drove them expertly back to the house, called 'Shamrock', in common with every place Aunt Bess put down roots. In accordance with custom, she took her nephew's arm as he crossed the threshold of her home (and an adventure no-one anticipated) and told him,

'You are most welcome in our home.'

Eddie, whose bungalow Roger had already discovered, was quite nervous of me, as I staggered over his doorstep with my rucksack getting heavier by the minute. I was touched by the way he welcomed me in, as the Irish always do, and immediately spotted the piano. It didn't look very used.

'Your friend's in the bath,' he said.

'Lucky devil,' I thought.

He showed me our room, which had a double bed, and I took off my boots with trepidation. A burst blister had turned into the most ugly

looking fold of skin in the middle of my left foot, between the hard
bits. I lay back, put my feet up on the bed and drifted through the
day's events.

We'd walked through the Wicklow mountains from Glendalough to
Knockananna, through the Vale of Glenmalure and some of the
loveliest scenery of our journey.

In the Vale of Glenmalure
The English came unstuck;.
Eight hundred died there, for sure,
When McHugh and O'Byrne ran amuck.

For me, the experience of descent into a valley followed by the climb
up the other side and over into a new vista was unexpectedly exciting.
We also saw the last of a mountain – the Sugarloaf – which guided us on
our first evening and through the trauma of the second day in Ireland.
We met the man who cut the grass at the sides of the mountain roads
from Glendalough to Aghavannagh, where the only refreshment was in
a cool fast-flowing stream. A little old lady gave us directions.

'You've walked from Glendalough? Now, that's good for ye. Walk
over the hill there and you'll be out of the Wicklow Mountains and in
Knockananna; and may God go with ye, lads.'

But for God, I wouldn't have been there.

'Your turn in the bath, Tone,' said Roger. 'I've left the water in – the
bloke said there wouldn't be enough for two.'

'Oh heaven, oh bliss, oh murky luke-warm bathwater.'

'How was the bath ?' asked Vera (known as Dumpsy).

'Fine and hot,' he replied.

*The two had already started to talk about their musical tastes. They'd
established that she played the piano and he, the trombone. Vera was
naturally very shy, but found it curiously easy to talk to Tony.*

*'John's at the door,' said Pets, who then whispered to Tony, 'John's her
beau.'Vera blushed, swallowed very hard and walked to the door to tell
John why she couldn't get away, with her cousin just over from Ireland. He
understood. She knew, however, where she'd prefer to be.*

*'Tony's been here five days and all you've done is talk. Why don't you
show him the riverside walk? Dumps ... Dumps! Can you hear me?'*

*'Yes, mother. How can Staines riverside be a patch on the scenery you've
told me about in Abbeyside, Tony?'*

'You'll be there, Vera.' It slipped out, unannounced.

They sat on a bench by the Thames. Without warning, he put his arm around her neck, drew her towards him and kissed her mouth, as lovers do: long and passionately. In a whole year, John hadn't done more than hold her hand. Not that there was any contest, but had there been, it was over.

She went into a spin; heartbeat, emotion, arousal and total reassurance. As for her suitor, he was overwhelmed. They looked at the river, but didn't see anything. The iron bridge needn't have existed. He kissed her cheek, then the other one, then her hand. Finally, he looked right into the biggest brownest eyes he'd ever seen and said,

'I love you.'

Eddie, our host, was watching RTE television with his two young sons Edward and Gary . He was pleased that we joined him in the lounge. His daughter Christine came in from her guitar lesson. We already knew about her: her father was obviously proud of her achievements in music.

'Do you mind if I have a go?' I asked.

We had a great session with all of us singing folksongs and popsongs. Even *Don't Cry For Me, Argentina* was included. We discovered that Eddie's wife worked shifts in the Braun electrical goods factory in Carlow, 20 miles away, and wouldn't be home until later. Christine brought us delicious home made soda bread and hot tea. I was impressed by her singing voice – strong for a ten-year-old. Her father was gentle and open. He told us that he rented a field from a local farmer and cut all his own turf for the heating of the bungalow and the cooking.

By this time, Roger and I were remarking on the air of resignation among the few Irish folk we'd talked with thus far. Fresh in my memory was the young barman in Fox's bar, Enniskerry ....

I want to work in a Union Bar
  In the centre of Dublin Town.
Your overtime's paid and you know where you are
  And the big man can't put you down.

Me pa has a farm in the County Kildare
  And I was the one to move out;
There wasn't enough for three sons to share,
  So I'll make my living from stout.

But, Declan, you're young and you're fit and you're well
  At the age of wonder and vision;
Living your days in the smog and the smell
  Can't be your only ambition.

You could go to Kilburn and shovel cement,
  Or even the USA,
And work till you're knackered and spend till you're spent,
  Or maybe you're better to stay.

So go and work in a Union Bar
  In the centre of Dublin Town,
But do look outside and see where you are
  Before your young life has flown.

When we left Knockananna, it was an unexpectedly emotional parting. We'd been touched by our hosts' hospitality and they had enjoyed our company too, it seemed. Christine was busily practising the finger-picking routine I'd taught her. On the road we discussed daughters, of which I have a severe shortage. Roger has a special relationship with his Susie, which is quite apparent when they are together. I love my three boys, but still make a beeline for everyone else's daughters: and I spoil them all! Our relationships with children affect us as much as those with adults.

'Shall we have children?' asked Tony.
  By the time their family noticed the blossoming of their relationship, they were already talking about the rest of their lives together. They were not secretive and, on the day her father returned on leave, the balloon went up.
  Sidney Smith was tall and straight as a soldier should be. A no-nonsense

Englishman, as tough on the outside as he was jelly on the inside and his emotions were seldom far from the surface.

'Mother,' (he always addressed Aunt Bess in that way), 'what have I come home to this time?

'What are you talking about, Sidney?' she said exasperatedly.

'Haven't you seen the two young lovers we've got under our roof? I saw them earlier. Eating each other, they were. It has to stop.'

Tony was forced to give up his job in Staines and dispatched back to Ireland, to face the music from his father. Vera was quite unable to hold back the loud sobs when they met secretly on their riverside bench to say goodbye.

'They can't keep us apart, love,' he said bravely. 'I'll make Dad understand. When he sees how much I love you, he'll change. Leave it with me.'

'They won't let you come back here, you know,' said Vera. 'When will I see you again ?'

'When I get back, I'll come to where you work. Don't worry, they can't keep us apart forever.'

I first met Eileen (my Dad's sister) when she was eighteen. I was eleven; waiting to start grammar school after the summer holidays in Dungarvan. I fell for her immediately and have never fallen out since. She and Ned (who was courting her then) gave us a marvellous time that year. We went to see *The Wizard of Oz*. The wicked witch gave me nightmares as I lay in the front bedroom of 789, New Line Road, asleep in the same house as two other Tony Andersons. I still remember my Grandfather's big nose, wooden leg, bicycle and violin, which he would play to my Mother's piano accomaniment. He suffered from asthma and so tucked the fiddle into his chest instead of his shoulder. He played in that sentimental Irish style which jerks the tears from the stoniest heart. Glory be!

It was Saturday. Every step Roger and I took was another three feet nearer to Dungarvan, Eileen and a restful break. Remembering strolls along the railway lines with Dad, I had a brainwave.

'If we follow the railway track, we're bound to arrive in Abbeyside,' I said.

Roger looked sceptical. As so often, the route had taken longer than we anticipated. We did follow the track, but we arrived at the disused bauxite works and the lighthouse at the northern end of Dungarvan Bay. I felt embarrassed and disappointed all at once. It put three miles onto our journey and, to cap it all, it started to rain. The bay seemed endless, but most of the landmarks were familiar and reassuring. In a way it was good that we approached Dad's home town slowly. There is a part of me which always says 'I belong here'every time I get anywhere near Abbeyside. Perhaps it's just romanticism; but I don't think so. I felt my friend's disappointment keenly. He wanted to see the bookshop in the town and it seemed possible we wouldn't get there before 5.30.

Eventually we found what used to be the Waterford to Killarney Line – now a footpath, thanks to an EEC grant. At Park Lane Green, Abbeyside, we received a real Irish welcome from Eileen and her daughter Emer. Ned and their son Keiron were out looking for us on the main road. It was a wonderful relief to be in familiar family surroundings, even though my feet were killing me! Roger saw the bookshop, while I chatted with Eileen and telephoned home. Emer was watching Laurence Olivier's film of Hamlet, which she was studying at school. Relatives arrived. I started to drift ....

Railway Children

Grandad was a railway child.
I'm beginning to feel inside
The rhythm of his life;
The changing points,
Buffers
And the grinding need to make ends meet.
Ireland doesn't compromise;
Nor does she take prisoners.
But, if you play your part
Correctly on Sunday morning,
You can get drunk on Sunday evening:
And Grandad probably did.

Dad was a railway child.
Poorly: member of the town band,
Who changed direction.
I'm beginning to see
What drove him away.
More important, however, is
That I know why he never came back
To stay.

I am a railway child.
Further down the track.
In a way, I am father to the other two,
As I broodily try to understand
Just how the trains ran
Without a timetable.

Tony walked down the track to Clonea, moving up the embankment as the 5.30pm express thundered past. He carefully rehearsed what he was going to say to his father. Surely, he would understand ?

'Out of the question.'

His father was definite.

'But Dad, I believe you can apply to Rome for special permission from the Pope himself. I love her, Dad: she is the one I want to marry. Please *accept that I love her. Can't you recall how you felt about Mother?'*

Hannah was quietly listening and praying. She remembered. It had been tough for them too.

'Your mother is not my cousin; to bother the Holy Father is out of the question. Your Uncle Sid has arranged for you to live in Hounslow. You can work there in the engineering trade, like John. Why can't you be like your brother, Tony? Go back to England. I forbid you to see any more of Vera. Your Aunt Bess will see to it. Be a good man, Tony, and God go with you.'

The reality was cruel. The family needed the money John and Tony would earn. As the express pulled out of Dungarvan and passed 789, New Line Road, everyone wept as usual. Nobody doubted the seriousness of the situation. Tony's heart was heavy. One face crowded his mind. His resolve stiffened. To defy his father was unthinkable. To lose Vera would break his heart. As he allowed his longing for her voice, her touch and caress to flow over him, the decision made itself. He dreamed of her lips, her eyes, her arms. He was heading in her direction and suddenly, that was enough.

Vera was working as a book-keeper and secretary in a London office. Copper-plate, hand-written, double entry accounts were the norm in the Thirties' business world, and she was good. She had concealed the turmoil within very well most of the time; but it was there, ready to rise to the surface. How long would he take? Would he give up? She even wondered if she'd imagined the whole thing. Then, suddenly, he was there, outside the office entrance as she finished work.

'Tony, Tony, I've missed you so much.'

They embraced, as lovers do. He held her close to him, enjoying the feel of her body against his, familiar and fresh, as though he'd always loved her; and was holding her for the first time.

Lyons Corner House in Charing Cross Road was relatively quiet. They sat in a nook and drank their coffee slowly. Tony gave her the bad news. She wasn't surprised. It was almost inevitable.

'You mustn't keep coming up here, Tony. You've a job to do. So how will we meet?'

They decided to meet at a teashop near Staines Police Station on Saturday afternoon that week. For Vera, it was half an hour's walk ; for Tony, a ride on the 117 double decker, and as he passed through Feltham that first of many Saturdays he wondered: would he ever go back to Abbeyside? Had he said all the wrong things to his father?

In O'Connor's Bar, they were warming up for an evening of music and drinking.

'Who's this?' asked Ned of an old Creamery worker, as he pointed at me.

'An Anderson. Tony Anderson's boy, is it?' (A fair bet, as I was with Ned).

'Sure I remember when your father would call in here for a pint on his way back from the crossing gates.'

'That was my grandfather,' I said, reluctant to correct him.

'And aren't you the very image of himself.'

Roger was observing patiently: but we were both finding it harder to drink any Guinness. After eight hours of walking, it slipped down effortlessly. After a (welcome) day of relaxation, it looked less appetising. The music was splendid: the company good and the band, which had a 65 year-old on the bodhrán and a 15 year-old virtuoso accordionist, sang our favourite song of the moment: *Fiddler's Green*.

Monday's parting was sad for me. Eileen and Ned took us into the main square of the town, where I posted various bits of extraneous luggage home and we transferred the poteen which Ned's nephew had acquired for us into smaller bottles. Then we headed up beside the River Brickey to Cappoquin and Lismore. When I was a child, Dad used to say 'Not so fast, you'll meet yourself coming back.' I felt as though that was exactly what I was doing.

The road to Cappoquin is gentle. It reminded me of the part of Surrey where I live. I imagined it as being like Weybridge before the developers moved it up-market into the stockbroker belt. Then we found the Blackwater River. Roger was unusually enthusiastic. Wide as the Thames at Twickenham, but empty. We discussed the possibilities for holidays afloat on the beautiful Blackwater. Would it just spoil its beauty? Of course, it couldn't become as congested as the Thames at Twickenham, could it? How do you balance these considerations? The discussion widened into an analysis of my characteristic ruthlessness (so-called). We found a way down to the riverbank, where we photographed the prospect of unsullied natural waterside. Even from a distance, with its spires and hilly aspect, Lismore looked tantalising. It didn't disappoint us.

As we passed the Protestant cathedral, which had an Englishness about it, we determined on a closer look, after we'd had something to eat. The town has an atmosphere of the drawing room of some down-at-heel, formerly famous Shakespearian actor. The second-hand shops displayed beautiful Victorian pieces at low prices but modern junk at much higher. We laughed and discussed the possibility of getting a van load of it through the customs and into the English shops. Terry's Hotel is in the centre of the main street – the frontage protrudes sideways, constricting the traffic flow. We entered, having already decided that, if the cost of B & B was more than £10, we'd soldier on. The proprietor was sitting at the bar drinking a pint of Guinness in the company of an elderly customer. Two charming young girls did all the serving. The B & B was a mere £8 each, so we joined the drinkers. I immediately noted the marble top to the counter. The hotel had undoubtedly seen better days. The owner began to speak, in a cockney accent. We learned later that he'd lived in London for some years.

'We'd like to catch a bus to Fermoy from here,' said Roger. 'Is there one tomorrow morning?' The old man smiled and looked into his drink.

'I'm sure there is.'

My companion and I looked at each other, wondering whether this was the truth, or just another example of a syndrome we'd grown quite fond of in the Irish. They tell you what they think will please you, even if it isn't really true! The boss told us to ask in Rose's West End Bar at the end of the street. The bus went from there, probably at 8 o'clock in the morning.

The Protestant cathedral was stubbornly closed, so we had a look in the Catholic church – a gaudy building, full of statues and pictures. It was obviously very active and powerful though it did not impress me. On one bank of the Blackwater is the Duke of Devonshire's castle. The walls drop from on high into the river like Camelot as I had always imagined it. We photographed. Roger enthused. We were captivated. Eventually, my complaints about being hungry were taken seriously and we found the Lismore Hotel on the strategic crossroads at the centre of town. The meal was pretty good. I had mixed grill. Then we found Rose's West End Bar.

She smiled at us in a semi-mocking fashion, which I attributed to the fact that I was limping from sore feet. It was Monday evening, 26 May and Rose seemed to take great delight in telling us that the next bus was indeed in the morning - Thursday morning! We were impressed by Rose, a sort of Diamond Lil, surrounded by youngsters who patronised the juke-box and played pool or snooker. There was a full-sized table in the rear. An entrepreneurial lady was Rose ....

Rose

Rose wears the trousers round here:
No cheques, no credit,
No taking a leer at her daughter.

Rose makes the rules in this bar:
So make sure you don't push her too far,
Or she'll blow you out of the water.

Rose is too good for this place;
And you won't stay long if she don't like your face.
So don't try to push her or fault her.

Rose has a furrow to plough;
The West End Bar is sufficient for now;
And the kids of Lismore will support her.

During a slow, painful stroll down the street towards Terry's, we 'phoned home, Roger infuriatingly unable to talk to Hazel, while I got through clearly. It troubled my friend for a bit. He was missing her organising of Bradford's part in a charity walk and wondering how the Quakers were doing. We entered what looked like the dingiest bar in Lismore and were greeted by what we took to be a husband and wife team. On the television above the shelves were the latest reports of the Rugby World Cup. As the lady poured our drinks, Pat came in for his usual.

'Good evening, Pat,' said the man as he took his eyes away from the screen. We could see he was elderly and almost blind – his eyes squinting behind a pair of beer-bottle lenses.

'Are you lads visiting?' Pat addressed us. For the umpteenth time, we explained the walk and its purpose.

'Do you know the Duke of Devonshire owns most of Lismore?' We looked inquisitive enough for him to get into full stride. 'Fred Astaire used to come here a lot. His sister married the Duke's son, you know. Fred was a mean bastard, but his sister was generous to a fault. She'd buy champagne and share it in here: but not Fred – he was a mean *******'

'Watch your tongue, Pat,' interrupted our hostess. 'Don't take any notice of Pat, lads, he's not short of a bob himself, with his garage business and all.' But Pat carried on and we heard all about the Devonshires and Astaires. The old couple told us they were the last of several generations of their family to own that bar and we concluded they must be brother and sister. I pictured Fred taking off his top hat, leaning his cane against the bar and tap-dancing his way across the room to tumultuous applause, in the days when Lismore was the place to be.

It was drizzling in Leicester Square. Tony took her arm and guided her through the crowd and past the newspaper stand, whose hand-written headline shouted of the invasion, by Hitler's forces, of Czechoslovakia. Vera was humming Begin the Beguine. *Not quite Fred and Ginger; still meeting only in clandestine circumstances, they turned into the Tube station and practically into the arms of Sidney Smith, on his way home from an army reunion.*

By the time they reached Waterloo and found seats on the Staines train, both Tony and Vera realised he was drunk. Booze rendered her father either fighting mad or soppy. Which would he be? she wondered.

'Well oi never,' came the Somerset drawl. 'How long has (hic) this been goin' on then?'

They explained, very slowly, to a rather disadvantaged listener, why nothing could keep them apart. Whatever anyone said or did, they loved each other and would never give in. So he might as well understand. By the time they reached Staines Central, they had an ally: and he was almost sober again, too.

At home, everyone was in bed. Their new found supporter decided to tell them of his exploits in Russia during the Revolution. Exciting though it may have been, they'd heard it before and had other, more pressing priorities, like if and when marriage, but he kept going, refusing to abandon his captive audience, until they were almost ready to sacrifice his blessing but not quite.

===

Ted Rooney is a poet. He told us so, before he attempted to bore us to death. We were a captive audience, imprisoned by exhaustion and sore feet at the end of our longest day's walk, under a hot sun, which had burned my arms and turned my face a shade of red it had never been before. Roger and I had begun to believe we'd never reach our target for the day, but there we were in Bunclody, B & B booked, facing real food and this American from the UCSB, which we took to be the University College of Santa Barbara. His hair and long beard were white, his wife, son and daughter-in-law quite charming, but he was the most incredible name-dropper we had ever met....

Pasta (American accent, first four verses)

Hi there, I'm from Santa Barbara, California
And I know Lawrence Ferlinghetti;
But before I go any further, I feel I ought to warn ya
That I talk in platefuls of indigestible spaghetti.

Allow me to drop the name of Gregory Corso.
Watch it ravioli down my long white beard.
For, you see, before I acquired the ability to bore so,
I had to learn how to look just slightly weird.

I recently went to a Gary Schneider launch.
It was instant recognition. Like 'Zap!'
He asked me how much pasta it'd taken to grow this paunch;
And announced he thought my poetry was crap.

I can drone on about Arthurian myths
Until the macaroni has boiled dry;
About ley lines and megaliths and monoliths
And how the English for 'ugh' is really 'why?'

So thankyou, Mr Rooney, for all your talking.
Just like that lasagne, it's repeating.
If my body would let me up and out and walking,
I could pay for all the garbage we've been eating.

Ted and his family were at the end of an expensive tour of Ireland. Americans tend to see things in terms of their monetary value and this latter day hippy was no exception to that rule. He ordered soup and sat opposite us in a place called The Fisherman's Rest on the edge of the main square in Bunclody. He let the soup go cold because he couldn't stop talking. Now and again, his son Michael would look either at his wife or mother and raise his eyebrows. He'd heard it all before.

Everything we drank disappeared without trace, we were so dehydrated from the walk, which started at just after nine in Knockananna and ended after seven, with no more than threequarters of an hour's rest. Our lodgings, Deanes, was not completed – even though a crowd was booked for the weekend following. Our room was comfortable: beds, dressing table, wardrobe and crucifix. Our first pint was in O'Connor's Bar. Mr O'Connor was wonderful, articulate and helpful: like his old pendulum clock, fully accurate and still advertising a brand of manure.

At eleven o'clock the workmen were still banging away at the incomplete guest-house. We were too tired to care and, with feet outside the covers to ease the pain, I drifted to sleep and dreamt about Gunnersbury Catholic Grammar School, where my companion and I first met. The Catholic artefacts around Deanes and a pamphlet about Padre Pio in the bathroom must have triggered something.

To me, Roger seemed very independent, able to do much more than I was allowed. I often felt isolated, indeed hated the place intensely, almost from the day I entered it, certainly from the day when the Latin Master threatened to thrash anyone who was unable to conjugate various irregular verbs. I refused to go to school, certain I'd be beaten senseless by a sadist who loved to strut up and down the aisles of the classroom singing Only Five Minutes More during a test, then whispering audibly: 'Who's going to get a thrashing then?' with evident and monstrous glee. I both feared and disliked Father Chapman and his horrid regime. In Roger, I discovered someone who thought a bit like me, whom I could both like and admire. In spite of ups and downs, periods of disapproval of each other, our friendship has endured as an enriching part of my life. I had shared the stage with him, when we played for Mick and the Backbeats and the Blue Diamonds rock groups and soon would share the back seat of the bus from Bunclody to New Ross.

We had to get to Dungarvan by Saturday. More days like the last one were out of the question, so we opted to bus to New Ross and walk to Arthurstown – a mere 12 miles – an afternoon stroll. I was excited at the thought that we were very close to Waterford City itself.

'Waterford has the best roads in the whole of Ireland,' Tony explained as he guided her around the city. The excitement and trepidation had made Vera seasick. Already she saw why Irishmen talk of the beauty of their homeland, but her first concern was the imminent meeting with her uncle, Tony's father.

'Mother, Dad, this is Vera.'

'Welcome to Dungarvan. Welcome to our home, young lady.' said Hannah. 'Tell us all about yourself.'

'She plays the piano, Mother.'

'Let her speak for herself,' said his father.

Within the hour, they were playing the first of many duets. Discussion changed from the marriage, permission for which was being sought from Rome, to the war, which Chamberlain had just declared.

'England is my adopted home, Dad. I've volunteered to join the army and will be going for the medical soon.'

'An Anderson fighting for the English. Who'd have thought it? Good man! Do what you think is right.'

'Take care. Don't get into anything foolhardy now,' said his mother.

They parted in the usual floods of tears. Back in England, Tony failed all the medical examinations. He had chronic kidney disease. It was unlikely he'd live beyond the age of 27.

November 23 1963 is the day when everyone remembers what he was doing, so they say. My dad cried uncontrollably as the news of President John Kennedy's untimely death came over the TV news. Although I joked about it to Roger, that was the scene in my mind as we passed the site of the Kennedy Memorial in County Wexford between New Ross and Arthurstown. It was a lovely walk, helped by a lady in a roadside bar, who provided cheese sandwiches and tea for two and charged us one punt. The estuary of the Barrow, with Ballyhack/ Arthurstown on one side and Passage East on the other, is gorgeous, and we saw it at its best, in the beauty of a red skied evening. Mrs Kennedy must have wondered why the family ever left County Wexford as she wept for her fallen son. Of course, it was their drive for fame and fortune that took Ireland's best away then as it still does (tragically) today.

The Youth Hostel at Arthurstown was a dump. Broken windows, lousy beds and cold water were only alleviated by a remarkable evening. It began at the local pub, where a group of seafarers were finishing a four-day booze-up. We were treated to some spirited singing, including *Fiddler's Green*, which Roger recorded on his micro-cassette machine. As we walked round to the Neptune Restaurant at Ballyhack, the deep crimson of the sky was reflected in the navy blue sea. We ate oysters and many different varieties of seafood in a converted schoolhouse. Apart from us, there was one couple there. It was, after all, a Thursday. evening. We went back to the pub. The seafarers were still at it. After 'phoning home, we joined them until closing time. The following day, as we took the ferry to Passage East and County Waterford, one of the revellers was standing on the quayside. Later, along the road, I spoke this poem into my cassette machine ....

Arthurstown Spree

With a face like a gargoyle, he stands on the quay
Coughing it up from his soul.
It's the morning after a four day spree,
And Guinness and whiskey are taking their toll.

Last night we watched as you sang us the songs
Of the bold men who set Ireland free:
Of brave men who died and righted such wrongs;
But today, there's a cold edge to reality.

We look from the ferry and there you remain,
Adding a sort of a hue.
If you're on the wagon when we come again,
We'll look at a different view.

For you'll be the country's next heroes:
You've paid the price of the past.
Whiskey and Guinness are zeroes:
Now sing us a song that will last.

Roger talked, with great affection, about his dad as we walked along. How difficult it must have been to consider the great philosophical issues of the day when life was so grindingly hard. In the First World War he was almost killed by an exploding shell. His comrades took him to the First Aid Post, believing him to be dead. He survived and returned to the front as a stretcher bearer. His health was permanently damaged: in later life, he suffered from chronic bronchitis and deafness. I remember so clearly his pipe (strictly forbidden), armchair and the pendulum clock in the corner. He'd often say something guaranteed to make me shiver. Once, he noticed my teenager's boil on the back of my neck and I wished I could drop into a hole in the floor. At first, he frightened me. Latterly, I too was very fond of John Jones.

It took Roger years to really appreciate his dad. An only child, with relatively elderly parents, he made a beeline for my close family environment, where there were four of us fighting for room. Mr Jones never voluntarily talked about his experiences in the trenches of France. I find it poignant and moving that brutality has such a dreadful effect on a sensitive man.

Sidney Smith put his arm around his daughter with strength and gentleness. Quietly, he told her what he knew about this progressive kidney disease from his time in the Medical Corps in the First World War. He wasn't famous for his tact: but his heart was in his mouth as he advised her:

'If you marry him, you'll be a widow before you're 25, Dumps, my love. One of his kidneys has gone altogether and the other is diseased. A man can live on one, but when that's gone, he'll die. Oh, Dumps, my poor little girl, I'm so sorry.'

'I want to marry him, Daddy. Even if I only have two or three years of happiness with him, that will be better than not having him at all.' The shy and quiet Vera had found a well of determination when she most needed it.

'Daddy, it was you who first realised we couldn't be kept apart, when you met us in Leicester Square. It's still true now, just as it was then.'

Giving his daughter in marriage to Tony Anderson on 6 March 1943, was the last public act Sidney Smith could manage. He died of cancer shortly afterwards, but he saw the victory of love over adversity and rejoiced.

Meanwhile, unable to fight, Tony was doing war work in the engineering trade. He'd become active in the Sheet Metal Workers' Trade Union, causing commotion when he called out on strike a factory which made heaters – because there was no heating and it was mid-winter. He read the standard works on Socialism, from Lenin to Sidney Webb and Keir Hardy, taking it all in, but never abandoning his faith in God and the Catholic Church.

'The sad fact is,' Roger said, 'that the Left has lost the argument in Britain. It doesn't matter what you and I may think, Mrs Thatcher's popular capitalism is what people want.'

During our trek, the British General Election of 1987 was in full flow. Neither of us was sad at the thought of missing most of it, having both been active in politics before. As the ferry from Arthurstown to Passage East reached its destination, we were both struck by the French appearance on the Waterford side. The weather looked menacing, for the first time in five days, and eventually, it did rain. However, by the time we had found and put on waterproof jackets and trousers, it stopped, mercifully, and the sun was out again. In retrospect, I am certain that our journey was made feasible by the fact that the weather was so unusually dry.

At some point during the late nineteenth/early twentieth century, somebody coined the ghastly phrase 'Emerald Isle', which the sentimental exile clings to and the tourist industry exploits. It represents Ireland as a land of mystery, romance, leprechauns and smiling peasants. By the time we had walked for a week, any influence from such advertiser's hyperbole had been ground out of us: and we were glad of it, for the reality is far more interesting and, in some ways, charming. One enduring memory is of the man who put a huge satellite receiver dish on the hill outside Dungarvan. He charges for a comprehensive portfolio of channels ranging from the four British and two Irish to some unspeakable international satellite programmes. All are cabled to your home for a modest monthly rental. His computer cuts you off, however, if you go two weeks overdue. This enterprising businessman's latest scheme is to manufacture the TV sets themselves. He calls them 'Daysho' - it sounds Japanese (although actually a pun on 'Decies', the Celtic tribe which formerly inhabited these parts) and helps boost the image.

Our target was Tramore by teatime. It was one o'clock, lunchtime, and we could see the spire of Tramore's main church across the bay. We found a roadside bar. It was locked and a fierce dog barked at us. We waited while the dog went on and on, realising that he stuck to the territory of the pub with his posturing. When the owners returned from shopping and opened up, we asked them whether it was possible to walk around the bay, to save trudging along the road. Typically, they advised us to hitch a lift. After the usual explanation, followed by the equally expected incredulity, they said nobody ever did it but, possibly, it could be done. Well, it couldn't be done. We proved it when we discovered that there was a river in the way. We went back to the main road rather dejectedly some hours later and got to Tramore just after the banks shut. Roger persuaded the Allied Irish to re-open and change some travellers cheques. I couldn't believe it: it gave us enough money for the week-end ahead.

We walked into a fairly well-to-do looking bar and were greeted by Duane Eddy's thumping *Peter Gunn*, which Roger and I played years ago. It was followed by a succession of Everly Brothers, Buddy Holly and Elvis Presley hits. We felt aged – some of these tunes are 30 years old. Refreshed, if jaded, we trudged on to Annestown. As we walked down the main street, we glanced here and there and then at each other. Roger had walked faster than I, as usual, and had already discovered the awful truth.

'The only town in Waterford with no pub, no cafe, not even a snack bar,' I gasped.

'The woman in the general stores says there may be something in the next town, five miles on,' said Roger.

'No thanks.' By now I was shivering from the fresh wind coming from the sea. We bought some bread and cheese, meat and yoghourt, sat by the road and ate it, while we waited for Eileen and Ned to rescue us. I felt cold, tired and just a little bit sick as my teeth chattered and I could barely contemplate ever moving anywhere ever again.

'I just feel sick all the time, doctor.'

'Is there any particular time of the day when it's worse?' asked Dr Leech.

'Let me examine your abdomen. Ah .... as I suspected: you're about six months pregnant, Mrs Anderson. Congratulations!'

Vera looked aghast. 'Doctor Leech?' Her bottom lip trembled. She didn't know how to ask him what, even to her, sounded like a ludicrous question for a married woman, but she blurted it out and the old family doctor laughed, held her tenderly by the hand and spoke softly:

'The same way it went in, my dear.'

The story went (as I heard it) that Doctor Leech had been a famous specialist and surgeon. Unfortunately, he had Parkinson's Disease, which rather curtailed his activities with the scalpel, but he could hit the spot every time with injections. His hand would approach you, shaking like a mad thing: then momentarily, he would gain absolute poise and plunge. After withdrawal, the shaking resumed. It was horrific, but we all loved him, with his pinstripe suit (including waistcoat and pocket watch) and stature of Winston Churchill.

Vera's blushes were ferocious. She felt hotter by the moment as she asked all the questions which her parents should have addressed years before. As she left the surgery, all she could remember was his instruction to drink a bottle of Guinness every day. She knew she hated the stuff; after all, she had been to Ireland.

'Three pints of Guinness,' said Ned to the old lady in the Bunmahon bar. I looked at Eileen, who was sticking to brown lemonade, and told her how good it was to see them. To me, she never gets any older or less lovely. The first pint went down without a murmur, but I was dreadfully exhausted and found it distressingly hard to keep to the subject. Roger and Ned were well away, leaving me to catch up with all that had been happening in Dungarvan. Eileen, of course, wanted to know about practically every step we'd taken.

The B & B was pretty up-market for us. On the television, in the lounge, was Gay Byrne, the most famous man in Ireland, with his *Late*,

Late Show. The National Lottery, tickets for which can be purchased everywhere, is drawn each week on Mr Byrne's 25 year-old show. One small sampling of this highly influential programme was disappointing. Lenny Henry was interviewed in a rather gentle, non-probing sort of way, simply to give publicity to his appearances in Dublin that week. The following morning found me describing an 'indefinable home-sickness' onto my notepad. Over breakfast of bacon, eggs, black and white pudding, sausages and tomatoes washed down with two pots of tea, we listened to the reports on the previous day's debates in the Irish parliament, known as *Dail Eireann*.

The issue of the moment was the impending referendum on whether or not Eire should sign the Single European Act in common with the rest of the European Community countries. The argument revolved around the question of Ireland's traditional neutrality. All the major political parties were in favour of signing, but the Workers' Party was against. So was Eileen – she would be campaigning that week-end for the following Tuesday's vote. Like many opponents of the scheme, she feared loss of the 'Irishness' of the country and its traditional values. The YES campaigners raised the spectre of lost EEC investment, the NO voters feared enforced membership of NATO.

It was a beautiful morning, the sea view quite breathtaking as we marched through Bunmahon and I waited for the pain in my feet to subside with whatever anaesthetic chemical one's body pumps into such regions. As I walked along, well behind Roger, through strong farming country and into the village of Stradbally, I mused about a married woman of 24, who didn't know about the birds and the bees until she was pregnant with my brother, who never lived to share my incredulity, nor even a day of life out of the womb, so I'm told.

Soon, Vera was pregnant again and, with the experience gained from her first sad encounter with childbearing, was eagarly seeking the wise old doctor's advice.

'Do you really have to hold your nose in order to drink the Guinness?' he asked.

'Then, please don't try anymore; I'll give you some iron tablets instead.'

At home, Tony tried to hide his anxiety with varying degress of failure. In her heart, she thanked God for every day her husband survived the ominous predictions. Gradually, their horror subsided. Perhaps it was a mistake, after all. Miracles do happen, don't they? Why shouldn't God provide one for them?

Five days before Hitler's forces surrendered, the child – Anthony Sidney, myself – was born. I weighed seven pounds and was named after my father and both grandfathers. My first four years were lived in the house in Staines, which was the family home during the war years for Tony and Vera, Aunt Bess, Pets and her husband Tom Anderson, Paddy and Tony's brother John and his wife Winnie. It was a big enough house. Indeed, the cellar was the air raid shelter for much of Richmond Road. In the darkest hours of the conflict, enduring friendships were forged in that cellar. I remember a musty smell, camp-beds with canvas stretched over wooden frames and gas masks and hurricane lamps hanging on the walls: and my first remembered Christmas, when Dad made a pedal car for me. It had a proper number plate, a door that opened, lights, a boot and perspex windscreen. I was over the moon at Father Christmas' generosity. Aunt Bess (whom I knew as Grandma) sang:

> *The holly green, the ivy green,*
> *The prettiest picture you've ever seen*
> *Is Christmas in Killarney*
> *With all of the folks at home.*

'Two singles to Killarney, please. Which platform is it?'

Roger and I made our way around Cork's railway station to the mainline platform. In due course, the train arrived and we boarded. It was very comfortable; opposite us were four companions who looked as though they were travelling west on business. We speculated that they were on Government surveillance, looking as they did, like posh Dubliners. The terrain was fairly boring, being flat and agricultural, until we saw, in the distance, the mountains of County Kerry. We were trying to identify them on our inadequate map when an intercom announcement told us we were nearly there. The decision to go by train from Cork to Killarney was made for several reasons. Firstly, we'd heard from Brian Richards about the *Cibeal*, a music and cultural festival, taking place the following weekend in Kenmare, and wanted to go. Secondly, there was no joy in walking more than 20 miles each day, making footslogging the entire trip too much. The train was a good compromise – we still managed over 200 miles on foot.

Killarney is very commercialised, but we found a reasonably priced tea and sandwiches lunch near the station before heading for the hills. Our target for the afternoon and evening was Black Valley Youth Hostel, on the other side of the Gap of Dunloe, between 12 and 15 miles away – quite a gentle stroll. Within 20 minutes walk of the centre of town we were walking beside the famous Lakes of Killarney, along the perimeter of the golf course, where American tourists can while away the hours humming 'If it's Wednesday, this must be Ireland.'

Soon, we were well off the beaten track, in a village called Fossa, whose centrepiece is a church, built in 1977 and dedicated to the Prince of Peace. The notice outside tells how the people of Fossa, under the leadership of their priest Father James Galvin, constructed the building in the cause of peace and reconciliation. Men and women from the island's four provinces, Ulster, Munster, Leinster and Connacht took part in the work and it is a tribute to them. Once inside, you are struck by the fact that, behind the main altar is a picture window through which can be seen the most gorgeous view of the hills surrounding. For us, it was a welcome peaceful respite after the bustle of the town and fury of the traffic near the big hotels.

Following the signs to the Gap, we started to climb. The sky was quite overcast, but never really threatened rain. In the cool late afternoon the walking was pleasant. Then a car came hurtling around the bend and, as it whistled past me, I felt the blast of cigarette smoke from its open window and heard its stereo booming as it skidded up the dusty road, leaving a cloud of exhaust fumes in its wake. I was angry.

'When I'm Prime Minister, or Tea Shop, as they say over here, people like that will be shot publicly,' I yelled at my partner, further up the road as usual. Out came my micro-recorder and in went this gesture of furious indignation ....

Cars

Cars are cocoons of the twentieth century,
Cigarette smoke at speed.
Aluminium and rubber, plastic and chromium,
Machismo, aggression and greed.

The man in the car with the CellNet telephone
Sips his Dom Perignon:
Takes a bite from his cheese-filled croissant
And a blast from Elton John.

In instant touch with the office,
In instant touch with his wife,
In instant touch with the whole damn world
But right out of touch with life.

The mountains and hills of West Cork and Kerry are special. They are wild and rocky, ruggedly beautiful and endlessly surprising in their colours and hues. As we climbed, the road started to become less well defined. I asked Roger if that was the Gap. It wasn't and when we were sure of that, then the next cleft must be it, we thought. We reached Kate Kearney's Cottage, where the road ends and (officially) only the ponies and traps, driven by their entrepreneurial jarveys, are allowed on and through the narrow mountain pass.

During the years prior to the Great Famine of the 1850s, men would stop at Kate Kearney's for a snack and some of her well known poteen. Not surprisingly, Kate was known as a great beauty, and we assumed that the poteen played a part in gaining her that reputation. After satisfying their thirst, the travellers would go on through the Gap. We decided not to break such an important tradition, and stopped for a pint. It was a slack day for the jarveys and they were playing cards in one corner of the cottage, which was named after Miss Kearney when it reopened for trade recently. Some of them were drunk, one seemed ready for a fight. We kept our distance and asked the lady who was selling souvenirs for a potted history of the place before setting off for Black Valley....

Silly Rhyme in Praise of Kate Kearney

Kate Kearney takes American Express.
I've been to her cottage and I tell you I've seen
The sign on the wall and the payslip machine
That say 'We're up-market and want to impress.'

When she was our flexible friend
At the Gap, where the wind can be bitter and keen,
She'd warm a man up, with a glass of pot'een
And put fire in his heart, as his way he would mend.

Our visa was having a thirst.
Her answer was Ireland's favourite beers.
And though Kate's been dead these one hundred years,
She takes the credit, for she was here first.

The breeze became quite chill as we approached The Gap. Derelict cottages told of an age-old struggle to wrest a living from these unyielding hills and mountains, a prospect which is sadly elusive. The road wound through the mountains, like the Yellow Brick Road, as we were to discuss later. My friend and I were enchanted by the beauty of it. The lakes, surrounded by outlines which became darker as the evening wore on, were magical. Each fresh vista took my breath away. Can one ever get used to this kind of scenery?

When we reached the hostel, after some tiring clambering (which did affect an unusually good short cut) we found it was crowded with teenaged Irish kids on a cycling holiday. We had bought some food in Killarney, knowing there would be no other way we could eat when we arrived, and set about preparing supper. Ingredients were: half a pound of mince, three big spuds, two carrots, one onion, one packet of vegetable soup. It was delicious – hot, tasty, slurpy and very filling. All around us, the cyclists were at various stages of their meals. In the corner of the common room was a turf fire, its characteristic smell inviting us to go and warm our weary limbs. After we'd washed up the utensils and plates, we went and sat by the fire with a couple of American girls and a German. They talked, while we wrote our impressions of the day. The teenagers were quite raucous still and we were getting pretty dopey. The fire crackled and I drifted in and out of a warm reverie.

My favourite childhood activity was collecting chestnuts, which we roasted on an open fire, in the ashes underneath the grate. Between Staines and Colnbrook ran Moor Lane, lined with chestnut and conker trees. We used to walk there on Saturday afternoons. My pedal car was converted so that my sister could sit in the back. We drove all around the council estate in Ashford, where we lived after the house in Richmond Road was lost to us. My mother hated it at first. For the first six months after our arrival, in 1949, she was so seldom seen by the neighbours that they assumed she was disabled. My dad worked at Copperads in Colnbrook, as a sheet metal worker. Already, his ambition was to start his own business and he took all new opportunities to gain experience.

With three children and a plan to get a new business going, Tony and Vera were so preoccupied that, even though they'd been warned, the trouble came like a bolt from the blue. The first holiday they could afford was on the south coast of England near Bournemouth and the New Forest. The caravan site was attractively set out in a circle, making the middle a good place for kids to play without getting lost – I can just remember it. There were good walks to High Cliff and the forest, which I found very exciting. We travelled by train, as there was no money for a car yet. Tony was feeling dreadful. He had a high temperature and splitting headache. By the time he got home, he was delirious. The family doctor called an ambulance. Vera looked at him, terrified. Was this it? Dr Whittaker had an exceptionally re-assuring air. Everyone seemed to trust his judgement.

'I think we're in time to cope with the fever. Just rest now, and go and see him later.'

The crisis passed and Tony returned after a couple of weeks. He looked thin and weak, frail and delicate. He was never the same again and they knew that their hopes of a miraculous cure were not to be fulfilled yet. As they sat by the fire Vera recounted the generosity of Tony's employer, Keith Wilson. As works manager Tony had gained a reputation as effective, honest and skillful. Mr Wilson had paid his wages and kept his job waiting. First for a couple of hours a day, then back to normal was the plan. The fire crackled, he dozed wearily. What would happen next?

Black Valley looked beautiful in the sunshine. Our target for Thursday was Sneem on the Ring of Kerry. First problem was breakfast. We had a little cheese and marmalade, so washed that down with the last two teabag brews Roger had left. Then we decided to raid the left-overs cupboard. In a green plastic carrier was a mixture of different sorts of seeds and dried fruit, each in its own little bag. In Ireland, vegetarianism is not exactly prominent. Indeed, the average menu assumes that one is a rampant carnivore. This didn't worry me much, because that is what I am. Roger had hardly eaten meat for a year before we set out, so he viewed our discovery with a little more enthusiasm than I could muster. No sooner had he started eating the produce, however, than a man appeared, whom we had only previously seen asleep, since that's how he was when we arrived at the remote valley the previous evening. He wore combat gear – a green jumper with shoulder pads and green water-resistant trousers. He had short cropped hair and was long and lean with green socks and army boots, which contrasted starkly with my mamby pamby Chris Brasher easy-life suede version. I guessed he was a British SAS man, getting away from it all in the Kerry mountains, as a welcome relief from the Falls Road.

He started to rummage through the cupboard, which in Ireland is called a press. As his eyes roamed here and there, I gradually cottoned on to what had happened. We had his seeds and fruit.

'Excuse me,' I said. 'Are you looking for a green carrier bag?' Roger was still merrily munching his way through a pack of sunflower seeds.

'Someone's taken it, by the look of things,' he replied in an educated London voice.

'Rog, could you give this bloke his breakfast?' I was pretty embarrassed by now.

'Sorry, we thought it was going spare, didn't realise ....'

He was very gracious about it all. We proceeded to eat toast while he mixed a cocktail of several types of seeds and dried fruit with Ribena. Aside, to my friend, I whispered the extremist word, 'Vegan', but was able to draw back from 'but then, he hasn't got pointed ears.'

We discovered that the mysterious stranger was a social worker from North London. He was hiking in Kerry, alone for a week, averaging six miles a day – a mere stroll. On the road, later, he stimulated a lively conversation (in his absence) about social workers and their problems, the fact that they are the victim of so many difficult situations and their general air of unreality.

The walk from Black Valley to Sneem was 20 miles. It took from about 9.30 am to 7 pm, with a short break at around lunch-time, when we ate some chocolate bought at the Youth Hostel washed down with lemonade. The countryside through which we travelled is unique in my experience, combining rugged beauty with gentleness in a way that defies description. In such surroundings, your thoughts readily turn to the mystery of Creation and how God speaks directly to each of us in the unity of what he has done. I also sensed the fact that what we see is the tip of the iceberg of God's handiwork, which is, indeed, marvellous. Here, we get to a point where Roger and I always debate furiously.

He sees the human race as an integral and, though important, not superior part of creation. Being an evangelical, I see man's role as headship over the other animals in God's creation. Well, you may think it's neither here nor there, but we can (and frequently do) talk about it for hours. It was the most Yellow Brick Road day of all, as the trail wound infinitely (it seemed) through the contours of stone, heather and green vegetation.

About two hours after we had eaten, while lying in a roadside field, we saw, ahead, a group of cars parked together. Our experience told us it was either a church or a pub. Soon we found the church but having received unreliable directions from a local cyclist, failed to find a bar. We walked for a mile, gave up the quest and returned to the junction, where a sign pointed to Sneem. About a mile further on, we found a blacksmith's forge, now overgrown, whose doorway was shaped like a horseshoe. We picked up little pieces of metal - evidence of activity long ago – and wondered what the place must have been like in its heyday.

Stan Cripps put a bit more coke on the flame. Then he turned on the electric bellows, so it made the fire glow with a brightness you could hardly look at without squinting. Into the fire went the point of a municipal pick-axe. Once it glowed sufficiently the old blacksmith would whack it accurately with his hammer, against the old rusty anvil. Very quickly, it was sharpened, dressed and quenched in a nearby trough. I watched, fascinated, as Dad talked business with Dennis, son of Stan and latest in a long line of Cripps' to work in the Bedfont Forge. Dennis was aware of more modern trends like mass production and, thanks to his father's enthusiasm, had been trained in the newer business methods but, at heart, he was a blacksmith in the forge that, so they said, used to shoe Dick Turpin's horse, Black Bess. Along with this story were tales of underground escape routes through Hounslow Heath, on which the old forge stood, where the infamous highwayman gave the slip to the forces of law and order. Like most lads of ten, I was with Turpin all the way, but Dad's call took me out of my reverie and into his Riley Pathfinder (a car, known to the family as 'Gremlin').

Tony was manager of an engineering company in Hounslow, which traded from a disused church building in a part of town to the rear of the High Street area. Its owner had spotted the Irishman's ability while he worked for Keith Wilson, and offered him a directorship. I accompanied my dad to the factory at weekends, so that we could prepare the Riley, a long, black, sleek, fast machine, for the trip to Ireland he had planned. Just inside the entrance was an enormous pile of junk, which had been there since before the War, and which Dad planned to move. I rescued a banjo from it, and taught myself to play Swanee River *and the like. The owner was Jimmy Redpath, a legend, as they say, in his lunchtime.*

We used to go for Saturday tea at 'Mr Redpath's' house in Henley-on-Thames. It had a tennis court of its own, a huge drawing room with grand piano and Persian rugs and seemed vast to us council house kids. There were even servants, including a butler/chauffeur, called Charles. He drove the Humber wherever Jimmy wanted to go, because his employer had a mysterious disability. My mother always looked askance at mention of Charles and the fact that Mr Redpath didn't drive himself. You see, during the War, he didn't fight. Instead, he accumulated enough wallpaper to make sufficient money to start several businesses when the conflict was over and the real shortages began.

Many years later, I needed a reconditioned three-phase motor and went to a shop in Isleworth. The man behind the counter asked me my name.

'Didn't you work for Jimmy Redpath?' he asked.

'No, but my dad did. I've got the same name as he had. He eventually set up his own business, you know.' He talked about the old days, one of innumerable who remembered my father: then he told me this – one more tale of dear old Jimmy.

'Your dad ran the factory in Hounslow. In the old days there was only direct current electricity, then it changed to 240 volts AC. I did the conversion on their motors, because Tony decided we were the best. Then the time for paying the bill came round. Mr Redpath appeared in the shop one day, right where you're standing. He told me that his business was about to go bust. I was practically in tears as I learnt how his wife had told him he must try to pay me as much as he could muster, because I was such a good and honest, not to mention charming, man. All he could raise, however, was ten shillings in the pound. I accepted, of course, relieved that I had, got at least half my money, thanks to dear Mrs Redpath. What I didn't know until later was that Jimmy then walked around the corner and into his chauffeur-driven Humber, ready to visit the next mug on the list.'

Eventually, Tony realised what was happening and determined to move on: this time, into his own business. At first, he couldn't afford his own premises, and had to share with Steve Gore in a corrugated iron shack near the river. It stank of soluble oil and Swarfega, because Steve ran a turning and milling business with his partner Bill, who had curly hair, a short-sleeved pullover and a dreadful stutter. Steve, however, was flash. He liked brassy women and, above his work-bench, there were pictures of them, with no clothes on at all. Tony used his skill as a sheet metal worker to gain a reputation for high-class prototype work. After some years of practice, he could turn a sheet of metal into any shape you'd care to describe, using little more than a series of hammers.

'What on earth is it?' asked Roger. The inscription next to the metal monument was written in Hebrew, Irish and, fortunately for us, English. Next to a sort of metal folded handkerchief was a plaque telling us that Chaim Hertzog, President of the State of Israel, was brought up here, in Sneem.

'My dad could have tin-bashed that monument,' I said.

'Let's find somewhere to stay. I'm knackered,' said my friend.

We booked into a whitewashed bungalow on the edge of town from which we had entered, showered (luxury), pulled on clean socks (heaven) and rested briefly on our separate beds (paradise) before making our way into the village in search of nourishment. Sneem is on the famous tourist attraction 'The Ring Of Kerry', a circular route through exquisite coastal scenery that runs 'the long way' from Killarney to Kenmare. These towns are, as the crow flies, 15 miles apart: as the tourist travels, however, it's well over 50.

Our first stop was a bar. No sooner had we received our Guinness than we noticed a picture of Ronald Reagan. Next to it was one of John F Kennedy. Stars and Stripes were draped around the interior and the large lady behind the bar had an American accent. We soon moved on and found a very clean, tidy and well organised restaurant. It was unusual for an Irish hostelry. In fact, it was Dutch. The food was tasty, the service excellent, the prices high and the quantity stingy, which the Irish never are, whatever their other shortcomings. As we left, not quite satisfied, we determined to find somewhere Irish, basic, real, working class, not tourist. Boy, did we find one!

On a bright spring evening, the only light came from the black-and-white television, on which the lovely and intelligent Olivia O'Leary (well-known among BBC Newsnight watchers) was fronting an investigation into the scourge of AIDS. Avidly watching this in-depth investigation were two middle-aged Sneemians, in brown boots and dirty blue serge trousers. The barman had a flat cap on his head and cigarette in his mouth. He was only just alive.

'Two pints of Guinness, please,' asked my companion.

We waited while he poured the drinks. It took ten minutes. Roger gave him a 20 pound note from our kitty. It took another ten minutes for him to organise the change. The beer was very cheap and undrinkable; we moved on to another bar.

Quite soon, being very tired, we got back to the B & B. In the lounge was a piano, which the daughter of the house played a little. What she did well was singing and playing the guitar so a short session ensued, encouraged by our charming hostess. Although it was very enjoyable, my fatigue began to overwhelm me. Without much persuasion I finished, exchanged encouraging remarks and went to bed.

I said goodnight to Roger and lay in that twilight thinking mode for a while. Tomorrow would see the Atlantic coast: then Kenmare for the Festival, on to Dublin and, by Tuesday, home. For now, however, a crazy scheme to cross a mountain and reduce a 21 mile journey to 12 was my main concern. Over breakfast, it seemed quite straightforward: by mid-day, it was less certain. Soon afterwards, we were lost in mist, on an uncharted mountain and soon, in the deepest bog we encountered throughout the whole journey.

At first, we just noticed the spongy nature of the ground. Then there were huge heaps of turf, or peat, everywhere and, whenever there was an isolated farm dwelling, the air contained the sweet smell of the stuff burning. Once in a bog, however, the exit is less easy. If you don't tread quickly, you sink. If you tread in the wrong place, you sink instantly, so you look for firm tufts of earth and move briskly.

The mist closed in and at one point we even lost sight of each other. Just as I was beginning to complain very loudly at my friend's inability to guide us to safety, we saw the Atlantic inlet, which ends at Kenmare. Below us was Castle Cove, so called because it is a cove, with a castle nearby. We didn't bother with that, making do with the small hotel named after it. In the bar, we were alone except for the barmaid and one other customer. While she got our food and drink, he started to gesture at us, grunting as he pointed at a picture of the local landmark.

'He wants you to go to see the castle,' said the barmaid. 'He's deaf and dumb, but can communicate.'

It took ages to transmit the simplest concepts, but we felt obliged to have a go. By the time we'd eaten our sandwiches, the afternoon was wearing on; having ascertained that there was no bus to Kenmare, we opted for hitch-hiking. At first, it was fun, but as the hours passed, we began to wonder at the wisdom of our actions. I found myself disconnecting from the situation and dwelling on my inner uncertainty. Roger talked to a shopkeeper about a taxi, to no avail. What if we don't get a ride? What if ....

I stood at the top of our road, waiting for the bus, which would take me to Ashford Hospital, where my mother lay, recovering from an operation. I was locked into a ring of uninformed anxiety. The most worrying aspect was that my Dad was so distraught.

Within months of his taking the lease to 1C, Station Road, Sunbury and moving a few basic bits of machinery in, Tony's world fell apart. Vera had cancer of the breast. Immediate surgery was the only recourse. Suddenly, it was all pointless. She told him he must keep going. She would get better. After all they had recently faced, why this? In the previous year, both Tony's parents had died - now he must face the possibility of losing Vera too.

After the operation came the radiotherapy: six weeks of being collected very early in the morning by an ambulance, driven to The Middlesex Hospital for radiation treatment and returned by early evening. Invariably, Vera felt dreadful at the end of each day. After the week-end break, she started to recover; then back to the sickness, tiredness and depression as another week took its toll. Eventually, it was over and we were able to have a holiday. Dad had taken a partner, for the simple reason that he couldn't cope otherwise. Walter Chessman was known, even by his wife, as Ches. He was warm, gentle, very big and strong. We loved him. Vera always thought the arrangement was a mistake. As with many things, she was eventually proved correct.

The holiday was in Somerset, in a beautiful village called Weddon Cross. There was a lovely black Labrador in the cottage next to the one Vera and Tony rented. The family visited Buckfast Abbey. After just over one week, Tony was in Minehead General Hospital, facing another crisis. The two or three days of 'touch and go' were horrendous. We children walked around the lanes. Then Aunt Bess arrived with Paddy. After the worst of the crisis, Tony's brother John went to the rescue and drove the family back to Ashford. After a few weeks, a frail and tired Tony arrived at Reading Station, where his brother met him and took him back to a big 'Welcome Home Dad' reception. After a week or two of Vera's care and cooking, he was back to work full-time again. They learned to look after him. He mustn't eat this, drink that, go there or fail to take various pills.

After a year, in which the couple began to build the business together,

their four children growing up and requiring typically vast amounts of
investment, Vera and Tony were almost able to forget their health problems.
Each of them attended clinics, to renew drug prescriptions and for checkups,
so obliviousness to the situation was not possible; but for them, these were
halcyon days. The family enjoyed holidays in Cornwall most of all. Land's
End and The Lizard were favourite places. Usually, a cottage or part of a
farm-house provided the accommodation. The journey took a whole day, so
an early start was essential. Once, when crossing Blackbush Airport, on the
A30, near Camberley, Vera turned to her husband and said:
  'I'm sure I left the gas on.'
  So we returned home, to find she hadn't left the gas on, she just didn't
remember turning the tap. As we laughed ourselves silly in the back of the
car, I could see, even then, the richness and joy of a relationship which had
so much more than its fair share of sadness and tragedy.

At last, Roger and I were in the back of someone's car: a Land Rover
with left-hand-drive. It collected us from Castle Cove after over two
hours' thumbing. It was a relief to be back on course, surrounded by
luggage, food and clothes, which belonged to the German girl who
drove and her pigtailed male companion. She had just completed a
horticulture course in Dublin and was having a last look at Ireland
before returning home. Her companion was over on holiday. They
were very friendly and helpful. What's more, they too were going to
the *Cibeal*.

The jeep stopped and our driver ran across the grass verge into a
field of what looked like weeds. She picked some plants and brought
them back to us.

'Smell those,' she beckoned, waving the weeds around. The sweetest
aroma of mint came from them. I was impressed with her ability to spot
the plants from such a distance. We drove through Sneem, where
Roger and I had spent the previous night. It looked strange from our
new perspective. Suddenly, my feet felt incredibly sore. It was as
though they knew their ordeal was almost over....

Feet

Father,
Thank-you for my feet.
I know I usually pamper them
And now, I'm abusing them.
But, by your amazing design,
They are coping.

Thankyou for the blisters
And the sore spots.
The tiredness,
The wonder of your creation and
Your fail-safe plan of redemption.

For, when my feet were hotly painful
And my sight was fading fast,
I knew you were there, because you said
'Those who trust in me for strength
Will find it is renewed.'
And it was!
Thank-you, Lord.

Our companions spoke perfect English, although they only used it when speaking to Roger and me. We, by contrast, had no German at all, so the conversation was dependent on the linguistic generosity of our driver and her friend. For us, this was the end of the walk proper. I felt a queasiness about that and whatever lay ahead, in Kenmare.

As Tony drove back past Blackbush Airport, Vera realised that they hadn't spoken for over an hour. Her stomach was churning at what she knew was almost certainly going to happen after she had seen Dr Whittaker the following week. The lump in her side was a tumour and she must undergo another round of treatment. For Tony, whom she spared the news until the last day of the holiday, it was what he secretly feared more than his own crises; losing the one who had given him everything worthwhile.

The surgery was once again followed by radiotherapy. This time, however, it was a little less crude, so less distressing. Ashford Hospital had acquired facilities for the treatment by then, so the arduous daily journey was eliminated. Nonetheless, it was one more in what seemed an endless series of ordeals. In my own stubbornness, I never thought of turning to God until I had exhausted my own resources. Why should I be surprised, therefore, that my parents took so long to actively seek two miraculous cures? That they left their four children with Vera's sister Mell and her husband Alg and drove through France to Lourdes, near the Spanish border, indicates how desperate they were to see middle age together. At the time, it was a fabulous adventure as they drove through several days and stayed in pensions along the route, while we children explored Muswell Hill, visited London, went to the pictures and watched television, completely unaware that our Mum and Dad knew they might not see us grow up, unless God would heal them.

Lourdes, in the Pyrenees, is the town where a little girl called Bernadette is said to have seen Mary, the mother of Jesus. Subsequently, faith in miraculous cures at the grotto associated with the girl's visions has turned the town into a point of pilgrimage for millions of Catholics and Bernadette into a saint, officially honoured by the Roman church.

Tony and Vera were greatly impressed by the evidence of previous miracles, in the simple belief of many very sick pilgrims, who were lowered into the water flowing from the cavern in which the Virgin is said to have spoken to the child Bernadette. They themselves bathed in the water and were the subject of prayer for healing. They attended candle-lit masses, which filled them with the wonder of God's love and mercy towards people who are often so rotten. They returned, refreshed, encouraged and closer to each other than ever. During another, all-too-brief period of calm, Eileen married Ned in Staines Catholic Church.

The reception was held in the house of Tony and Eileen's sister, Mary. The whole family turned out, enhanced by many of Ned's relatives from Dungarvan. One of the guests was a priest. He ran the town band to which both Ned and Tony once belonged and was much loved. I soon found out why, as he organised the evening's entertainment. Everyone did his, or her, party piece as usual. The special part for me, however, was that it was the first time I'd heard traditional Irish music played well. My dad sang The Mountains of Mourne *with feeling. I was proud of him.*

'I thought you played *The Mountains of Mourne* really well on that piano in Sneem last night,' Roger said unexpectedly, as the Land Rover pulled into Kenmare's market square.

'Dad used to sing it as his party piece. It's very special to me. That was a good session we had, last night.'

We thanked our German hosts profusely, saying we'd buy them a drink during the weekend and started to look for somewhere to stay. We settled for the attic room in The Shamrock. It had two clean beds, a wardrobe and wash-basin. As soon as we'd settled in, we decided to find out all about the festival. A free news-sheet told us a little about it, but we weren't really on the wavelength of folk who went on about Sweeney, a legendary Irish king, who turned into a bird and whose profile (post-metamorphosis) was the *Cibeal*'s logo.

Most of the events were held in bars or hotel ballrooms. We were fascinated by a series called 'Flying Solo'. It included a talk on trees, which we attended, a poetry session and a talk on astrology. They all started late, as did the concerts. All around, in the streets and bars, were *ad hoc* music sessions. At one point, a rock group got going in the main square. We soon realised (and were not even slightly surprised) that the festival was a terrific booze-up for all involved and watching. We ate, rested and set off 50 yards down the street to see and hear Jimmy McCarthy, a singer-songwriter in the Chris de Burgh style. He was very good. The bar in which he appeared was packed. People talked and drank while he delivered songs with a wide variety of interesting lyrics. The PA system was loud enough to drown the noise of a pneumatic drill. This was the end of a day in which we had been lost in the mist on a mountain, walked an unknown number of miles through bog and forest and hitched to Kenmare. Megawatts of sound were probably not what we needed most at that juncture (well after midnight), so we retired to our room in the roof of The Shamrock, to sleep, to dream of home and to prepare for another exhausting day of Irish festival.

Saturday began with breakfast of fruit juice, cornflakes, bacon, egg, sausage and fried bread washed down with umpteen cups of tea. Suitably gorged, we headed, gently, for the Kenmare harbour. Along the road were folk camping for the duration of this special week-end. They seemed to congregate wherever there was a sign which prohibited their doing so – another charming Irish characteristic which I frequently exhibit. The scenery around the Atlantic inlet is not easily confined to words. Whenever I visit West Cork and Kerry, I experience the same movement in my spirit when I look at the mountains in their richness of colour set against the blue tones of the sea. Soon we met Brian Richards again and started doing the rounds of *Cibeal* events.

The talk on trees was given by an Englishman who had been a resident of Glengariff (in Bantry Bay) for 15 years. With great

114

enthusiasm, he told us that a Tudor man o'war was built at the expense of 2,000 oak trees from the area of Cork around the River Lee, where the best quality ones grew. We heard the arborial history of Ireland from 15,000 BC to the present day. The chief slogan was 'Eucs, not Nukes', and we heard the praises of the monkey puzzle tree sung as a means of re-populating the country with timber. This, we believe, is it! Two more pints, please.

At the Park Hotel was an exhibition. We didn't get to see it, because there were far too many pseuds in the way of the paintings. The room, in which the art was displayed, contained so many people holding glasses of fizzy wine and plates of crudités that you couldn't get in. The place was full of self appointed critics who wouldn't, one suspected, know a decent picture from a hole in the ground. Anyway, it was far too posh for us, in our rough walking attire.

By early Saturday evening, we had sat on the kerb-side drinking Guinness, visited various aspects of the festival and chatted at great length about the meaning of life. We had already purchased tickets to see Jackie Daly, Kevin Burke, Arty McGlynn and Andy Irvine, collectively known as Patrick Street, in the evening, so we decided to rest until the concert was due to start. This time, we expected the advertised 10.30 start to be optimistic and set out at that time. In fact, the show started at midnight. We thought there was probably a good crack ahead. Patrick Street had been the guests of Gay Byrne himself, so they must be pretty special. As we crossed the Kenmare suspension bridge, on our way to the concert, at 10.30 pm., the sunset was not quite over, so we stopped on the bridge and gazed at the Atlantic and what remained of Saturday 30 May .....

Prince of Peace

'I have yet one more delight
For your eye today,'
Said the Lord of Lords
'For you who will look to sea.'
And, in the wild west of Ireland,
The peace of Heaven touched the water.

The untamed mountains
Became charcoal shadows
On the ocean's edge.
So we stood on the bridge,
Breathing the view,
Until the joy of Heaven filled our souls.

The return journey was different. Instead of the embers of an extraordinarily red sunset we were treated to the revelries of hundreds of drunken Irishmen, some of them actually tightrope-walking the suspension bridge supports. The concert had been excellent: top quality traditional music. At 1.30 am, there was an interval. Roger went back to the hotel to see if we needed a pass-key to re-enter. He was told we must be in by 4 o'clock or risk being locked out! When he returned, I was able to tell him that an announcement had just been made to the effect that the bar would shut as soon as the concert resumed. In the event, it remained open for the duration. The customers gaily staggered back to the town centre. We felt desperately sober in such company. Back in town, the festivities were still in full swing; and it was 3.30 am. In The Shamrock, the party was going strong. We went to bed in the midst of a town determined to reach oblivion and stay there. I dozed off, feet still tapping.

'I wonder if they sell the English Sunday papers here?' Roger grunted a reply which indicated that he didn't much care. It was 9.30 am when I ventured back into the streets of Kenmare. They were still drinking, singing, staggering and playing. To my eyes, it looked a trifle sordid. I bought the Irish papers, since ours didn't get that far west, and returned. On the door of The Shamrock, a man had been posted to prevent people too drunk from entering.

'I'm staying here,' I said, panic rising fast. He let me into the hallway. In the bar, at the end of the hall, they were still drinking. We had breakfast and prepared to leave. Our plans were vague, but they materialised marvellously, as Brian gave us a lift to Killarney in a borrowed car and we caught the train from there to Dublin. In Killarney, we bought *The Observer* and *The Sunday Times*, which contained a small job advertisement I wrote before leaving England. What a way to be reminded of reality! Before catching the train, I telephoned Eileen to thank her for the previous week-end. We had a long chat, for a 'phone call. It reminded me of when she and Ned lived in England.

Next to the workshop in Station Road, Sunbury was the estate agent's shop through which the leasing was arranged. Tony knew the manager well and, when the flat above the shop became vacant, secured it for his young sister and her husband. Ned worked part-time in the factory making the fluorescent light casings everyone involved with the business came to know and love. Vera returned after her second operation and became even more involved with everyday company activity. Tony secured the business of several large firms and, with it, an unprecedented degree of security for him and his family. He bought a Humber Hawk, his dream car, and began looking for a house. In their moments together, in the evening, he and Vera planned their future: financial security, their own home and their children grown up and settled.

Doctor Royds was unusually straight with Tony that day. Outside, in the car, the family was waiting for a treat outing to the pictures. He sat in the driver's seat of the Humber, tears streaming down his face. Everyone stared. What was wrong with Dad? The film was Rio Bravo *with John Wayne, Angie Dickinson, Robert Mitchum and Ricky Nelson. Tony enjoyed westerns; he always had, since coming to England before the War. This time, the specialist's words wouldn't let him escape.*

'There is a definite deterioration in your remaining kidney and, since you only have one, I must advise you that the situation is very serious.' What about his plans? No-one would grant a mortgage to such a sick man. After Robert Mitchum had sobered up, Angie Dickinson had fallen for Big John and Ricky Nelson had sung the song which lifted the spirits of the heroes enough to enable them to free the town from the bad guys, Tony told Vera what he had heard that afternoon.

'They've been telling me I'd lose you since I first loved you. We didn't give up then and we're not giving up now.' They cuddled in front of the fire, to the embarrassment of their children and toasted the future in Harvey's

Bristol Cream. Vera rarely wept. She didn't know this time whether her tears were sadness at his news or joy that he was over 40 and still alive.

Our fortieth birthdays, like all the others, came within five weeks of each other for Roger and me. We had intended to mark the occasion with a trip away together. I was struck down with back trouble and hospitalised during our fortieth year. As we sat on the train to Dublin, I reflected on what we'd seen during two extraordinary weeks since leaving Heathrow and wondered why the old bloke behind us was swearing so profusely. Soon, it became quite apparent that he was drunk. His companion, with whom he was holding a sort of conversation, sat two seats forward in the opposite row, while the swearer was immediately behind us.

'I wish I'd never ******* met you. You're a complete waste of time. You're wrong about everything. You're a complete ******* idiot, sure you are and no ******* mistake.'

His companion was a bit more coherent. He asked what on earth the other fella was on about, upon which the first fellow became humble.

'You're quite right altogether. Sure, I didn't know what I was talking about. You're a ******* idiot anyway.' So it went on, for ages. At first, we were amused, then slightly irritated. The train itself was excellent: quiet, comfortable and clean. It rode into Dublin's Heuston Station and we were back to where our journey began, to spend 48 hours having a look at Eire's capital city.

Though the trek from the station to Mountjoy Square took us along the Liffey and down the famed O'Connell Street we were pretty miserable by the time we had completed what, for us 200 milers, was an amble, and were cold and depressed. It was the Sunday of a Bank Holiday week-end – drizzling rain permeated both the atmosphere and our mood. Soon, we determined to telephone Aer Lingus and ask to go home the next day. An answering machine told me to try again at the following 8 am. Only a couple of pints of Guinness in a bar off O'Connell Street and some good conversation with my friend were able to relieve the gloom.

'Do you remember the school trip to Italy?' Roger asked, unexpectedly. We had been admiring the timber and glass Victorian decor of the Dublin bar, so I was required to do some rapid recollection.

'I remember the awfully long train journey from Calais to Rome, the plains of France and the beauty of the Alps. I remember the Vatican and St Peter's Basilica. Even then, I was outraged by the vast wealth of the Church and poverty of the people around. Everything tasted of olive oil and we were looked after by some nuns, who also used too much olive oil.'

We recalled illicit evenings smoking Lucky Strikes and drinking the local plonk. One night, we were chased back to barracks by angry teachers. As usual, one or two of our accompanying priests got drunk. As we laughed, once again, at these antics which, if perpetrated by our own children would send us into apoplexy, I remembered the scene to which I returned, full of stories about Italy.

Tony had been through another crisis. This one the worst yet. He almost did not survive. It was shattering for the whole family, and I felt terribly guilty about missing it completely. Vera's health was good at this time, but the latest bout had coincided with the break-up of Tony's business partnership with Ches. Tony's brother John helped out in the factory until recovery was complete. Once back at work, he bought me a guitar from a second-hand shop in Sunbury. The condition of ownership was that I mustn't give up playing violin in the orchestra and school ensemble. Roger and I started Mick and the Backbeats, followed by The Blue Diamonds, as whom we spent two weeks in Jersey. So, while I roamed, the fiddle burned and, one ignominious Tuesday, was told not to return to my tutor until I could play the arpeggio of B flat minor with complete fluency. He never saw me again, and I have regretted it many times.

===

'Start spreadin' the news (da dadada da da dadada). New York, New York', came up the stairs of the Mountjoy Youth Hostel at a rate of decibels. Frank Sinatra found us in uncomfortable top bunks at 8 am on a drizzly Dublin Bank Holiday. The dormitory was almost full and we decided to sleep elsewhere on our final night in Ireland, once Aer Lingus had assured us that there was no hope of returning to England before Tuesday, our appointed day. Having booked tickets at the famous Abbey Theatre for a play called *Say Cheese!*, we embarked on a tour of the city.

Trinity College library was shut, to our dismay, but we had a good view of the University buildings. In St Patrick's Cathedral, Ireland's first Christian site, we saw the influence of the great Dean Jonathan Swift, who sat in an enormous wooden chair and invented Lilliputians. By this time my nose was peeling as a result of the sunburn acquired between Knockananna and Bunclody. It looked quite sore and caused a little girl to comment. After explaining why church organs sound so eerie (she thought the Holy Ghost was playing it), I turned to face this outspoken eight-year-old.

'Your nose – what happened to it?' she exclaimed.

'I was in a fight – you should have seen the other bloke,' I lied.

Soon Roger's cold-sore had been attributed to the same battle and she and her friend were telling us how bravely they would have supported our cause by pulling on the legs of our assailants. Afterwards, at their request, we took photographs to post to them later. Their boldness in approaching us pointed once again to the difference between Ireland and England where children are concerned. How sad it is, we reflected, that this acceptance of them as part of everyday activity is overlaid with (often necessary) suspicion in England. We were cautious at first in our response to these two children because of our English conditioning: 'Don't talk to strange men.' Few can have looked stranger than we did.

Near the Mansion House was a second-hand book fair. Needless to say, Roger wanted to have a look, compare prices, generally browse and do what booksellers such as he do. My stamina for this event was lower than his, although I enjoyed a good thumb through some interesting stuff. There was a volume on the Constitution of The Irish Free State, which was far from tedious and quite enlightening.

No Irishman is immune from the consequences of the declaration by Patrick Pearse, on Easter Monday 1916, of The Irish Republic, when the green, white and gold tricolor was raised above the General Post Office in what is now O'Connell Street. The subsequent battles and talks led to the Free State compromise of December 1921, whereby Ireland remained in the Commonwealth, the Crown was Head of State and the small group of Protestant loyalists in part of the province of Ulster, would gradually be accommodated, reassured and assimilated. Beside the Free State document was the Constitution of the Republic, dated 1937. The nation would be called Eire and would include all four provinces; Ulster, Munster, Leinster and Connacht. Its government would be democratic, elected by the single transferable vote system, with two houses of parliament, the Senate and the *Dail Eireann* and an elected President. The first was Mr Eamonn DeValera of *Fianna Fail*. The first language of the Nation would be Irish.

As a child, I was taught the names of the six counties of which the Republic had been deprived. Since then, we have all seen the consequences of putting our political ideals above concern for the lives of others. Nonetheless, reading these noble sentiments of Eire's founders and feeling the anguish of that 'Unfinished Revolution', of which Christie Moore's new album speaks, fills me with a mixture of indignation that such a lovely island cannnot find peace, and despair that she ever will.

> And then I prayed I yet might see
> Our fetters rent in twain,
> And Ireland, long a province,
> Be a nation once again.

We all sang the chorus with gusto on New Year's Eve 1963:

> *A nation once again,*
> *A nation once again,*
> *And Ireland, long a province,*
> *Be a nation once again.*

As often before and since, Ned was in charge of the community and solo singing activities. He went on to give us Paddy McGinty's Goat. *Tony and Vera sang* I'll Take You Home Again Kathleen. *I could only manage something by Lennon and McCartney, a new and popular songwriting duo.*

At that time I was reading the great Russian authors: Tolstoy, Turgenev, Dostoyevsky and, with great enthusiasm, Lenin and Trotsky. Books like The Immoralist *by André Gide influenced me and I passed many of the midnight hours arguing at great length with my dad about the big issues: death, God, Socialism and Capitalism. He was the perfect opponent, always ready for more, never willing to concede. Already, we were becoming more than just father and son and our friendship grew through that year. I couldn't understand why he and my mother should cling to a God in whom I was losing faith rapidly. Much later, I saw the error in this, just as in the abandonment of the violin: but God forgives.*

One Monday, in early February, I asked Teresa West if she'd like to go to Eel Pie Island to see Long John Baldry. To my great joy, she agreed. The interval act was a bloke called Rod Stewart. Everyone called him 'Rod the Mod' because of his bouffant hairdo. By now, I had Teresa's 'phone number and was able to call to arrange a second date. We shared an evening with Roger and Hazel.

Roger had made several attempts and so had I. Perhaps Monday is a bad day to telephone from Dublin. Perhaps Bank Holidays cause congestion. Anyway, this time I did not get through to Teresa: our son Matthew took the message that I would telephone from Heathrow the following afternoon. By now, much of the city was becoming familiar. We were registered for the night in the second Youth Hostel, slightly out of the centre, and were ready for our evening at the theatre. In our dormitory, an Australian was telling an American about the wonders of cricket.

'Those guys play for five days at a time? It seems so slow.' He was assured that it is a great game, mate.'

The play was funny but average. It concerned marriage and the conventions surrounding it. The Abbey was surprisingly provincial in atmosphere compared with the National, Barbican or West End of London. The auditorium was almost full, but the preponderance of American accents made us wonder if the tradition which spawned George Bernard Shaw, James Joyce, Sean O'Casey and Oscar Wilde was as strong as ever. Back in the hostel, after a drink and the bus ride home, we were settling down for the night. In the period of half-sleep, I was imagining home and loved-ones and remembering our arrival, sixteen days previously. Then the Australian arrived back. For an hour, he described in great detail the ten pints of Guinness and innumerable glasses of Jamesons whiskey he had consumed. We were desperate, but silent. Eventually, we slept and, the following morning, made our way back to the centre of the city after a meagre breakfast.

After depositing our rucksacks in the bus station luggage store, we parted, to spend the last couple of hours in Dublin collecting gifts, previously undesirable, because they would have to be carried. It poured with rain for most of the morning and I longed for home as I dodged the traffic and tried to miss the parts of the streets most affected by the rain. In the shops, there was tourist junk – folk dolls, shillelaghs (we'd been there) and leprechauns. Eventually, we kept our rendezvous at the bus station and rode to the airport. It was almost certainly our enthusiasm that got us there so far ahead of schedule, but we had lots of time in which to ponder, talk and daydream. I daydreamed.

Our Boeing 727 moved slowly down the runway. The stewardesses walked down the centre aisle, their eyes glancing this way and that in search of an unfastened seat belt or unextinguished cigarette. The silver monster, with a shamrock on his tail-fin, turned sharply, then came that surge of immense power in the back, forcing us against our seats as the jet engines roared. Out of the window, the ground moved ever more quickly underneath until it was a streaky blur. I was aware of having lost contact with the ground just before I lost consciousness .. .. but the stuff of my reverie was the reality of Sunday 17 May and the flight in the opposite direction. Soon, I would awaken on the approach to Heathrow and home but, for now, I replayed the outward journey and, as never before, the final part of the story of my parents, Tony and Vera.

I had a streaming cold throughout the week before the journey began. The flight was comfortable but we had spent much of it lamenting our selfishness, not to mention foolishness at embarking on such a project. We had set out from Marlay Park at about 5.30 pm., intending to reach Knockree Youth Hostel by 8 o'clock. The Wicklow Mountains rise sharply on the south side of Dublin and I was wearing a waxed waterproof coat under my heavy rucksack. Forty-eight hours later, I had abandoned such superfluous weight, but now I was to pay the price of going straight into a long walk unprepared and with a heavy cold. After 20 minutes hard walking, my corduroy shirt (another mistake) was soaking wet with perspiration. I felt the panic rising.

'I'm going for a swim.' Tony's pyjamas were soaking wet with fever-induced perpsiration. Vera had seen him delirious before. The whole family knew the signs. He always wanted a swim. We'd joke about it later – after all those years by the sea in Dungarvan, he'd learned to swim in Hounslow swimming baths. Vera was praying. Soon she was on the 'phone to Father O'Callaghan, their friend and parish priest. He would say mass for Tony's recovery.

For the first time, now that Ches was gone, I became very involved with keeping the business going, contacting clients and working in the factory to complete orders whose delivery schedules were always very demanding, in the cause of competitiveness. My entire knowledge of engineering was gleaned from my Dad. Later, I went to Polytechnic, but for now, it was hit and miss. We survived. The bronchial side of my father's trouble kept him from work for over six weeks, including a spell in hospital. It was discovered, during that stay, that his heart was being damaged by the kidney's malfunctioning.

It often seemed then, and even more so in retrospect, that whenever Tony and Vera's family had enjoyed more than a few months of what passed for normality, tragedy struck again. May, June and July 1964 were wonderfullly calm. After the end of term, I worked with my dad and travelled around with him in the Humber. It had a radio on which I could listen to the exciting new pirate stations, while he was talking to a customer or the bank manager. On one such occasion, while browsing in a second-hand bookshop, I found a novel entitled Peace In Nobody's Time. *Later, it became* Bolonia, *a musical by one Mike Carter and me. We even met the book's author, George Borodin.*

'Do you think you'll do *Bolonia* again? asked Roger. I was fighting fatigue, despair and sickness and he wanted to talk about that. The concentration was good for me. The terrain was changing for the better and we could see the mountain, whose characteristic shape could be seen in a photograph of the place to which we were walking.

'I hope so,' I replied, while thinking, where am I? 'It will need quite a bit of re-writing, so goodness knows when.'

The perspiration was making me shiver now. Sneezes followed. We turned to each other, realising that we were lost. Ahead was a bog: beyond that a road which, we reasoned, must go somewhere. The first two days were very tough for my friend too. He became convinced that he had dragged me all the way to the wilds of Ireland to watch me collapse. Without his help, I wouldn't have survived. That first evening, he kept talking.

'Oh, by the way, Tone, I think your new musical about Mary is great. The words and music fit well.' We went on to discuss his book *Green Road to Land's End,* which is my favourite. He told me of his adventures while researching his book on the Bristol Avon and how his first, a town history, is still selling well. Knowing we were about to enjoy two weeks of discussing anything under the sun (and we did) lifted me during those first critical ten miles, which I reckon were at least 12, allowing for bogs, detours and Fox's Bar.

'Just one, that's all.' We agreed solemnly. Inside, the band was setting up and testing its PA system. I couldn't believe my ears, when I heard:

> I don't care if the weather freezes
> As long as I've got my plastic Jesus
> On the dashboard of my car.

'Rog, Rog, did you hear what he just sang?
'Maybe you misheard, Tone. He *is* Irish.'
'Is this the only bar here?' I asked Declan, the Union Bar man.
'No. In fact, you're paying extra here, for the music.'

'We're paying extra for the music? You're not serious. Rog, did you hear what he just said?' In the snug bar, we were able to order two cheese sandwiches each. Roger suggested we kept half of one of them in case there was no food at the hostel. In the event, it was a very wise move. Our vow to have only one pint of Guinness held sway until the second, whereupon we submitted to the charms of the black liquid and had one for the road.

By now, it was dark, but we had been given directions and felt much better as we developed the rhythm of a marching step. The sky was navy blue, rather than black, and for the following three hours, we were sure our destination would be just around the next bend in the road.

_____

Hayling Island, on the south coast of England would be ideal, Tony thought. Inexpensive, close to home and a place big enough for everyone. Roger and I hitched or, more accurately, walked, hitched and caught the train. Following several drinks in Chiswick and Staines, we got a lift from an A.A. van. He took us to a spot just outside Farnham, where we slept in the undergrowth, covered only by the glow provided by a few sips from a flask of whiskey. In the morning, we woke to the sound of a milk float, ran down the embankment and hailed the driver. He practically died on the spot, but agreed to sell us orange juice. After a fruitless period of thumbing on the Farnham bypass, we caught the train to Havant and bus to Hayling.

The bungalow contained Tony and Vera and their four children, John, their daughter's boyfriend, Roger, and Teresa at the weekend. Tony was, by now, much better and Vera felt more healthy than at any time in five years. Even the weather was good. We all joined the Beach Club and spent happy hours doing nothing in particular. We played the guitar and sang and played cards until late at night. Roger and I slept in a tent on the lawn.

_____

Knockree Youth Hostel was cold, noisy and uncomfortable; but it was the place where we were supposed to be. As yet unused to the rigours of hostelling, I chose too few blankets and suffered. A dog barked for much of the night and I found it hard to believe that so little time had elapsed since leaving home. The following morning saw us sharing hot water with some school children and scrounging some milk for Roger's teabags. The half cheese sandwich was our breakfast. We set out for Glendalough, along the Wicklow Way, with the vaguest of maps, too much baggage and a small flask of whiskey.

_____

'*Are you Mr Anthony Anderson?*' asked the policeman.

'*Yes, I am.*'

'*Do you have a factory in Sunbury-On-Thames?*' he continued.

'*I think you want my father. That's him, over there, on the beach.*'

Tony looked at the damage with utter disbelief. The fire had clearly started at the rear of the building, spread slowly and caught the gas main, at which point there was an inferno. Water had caused as much damage as the fire itself and one of the firemen had lost a hand in the blaze. Why should this happen now?

The insurance people were unable to pronounce on how long it would take to process the claim. In any event, he was greatly under-insured and would receive scant compensation. It was the first time he had closed the place completely for the holidays. Previously, he and Ches had staggered their breaks so that it was always open. With Ches gone, this seemed the most sensible. Was it arson, committed by naughty children? No-one could do more than speculate. By evening, he was shattered and ready to drive back to Hayling. Just outside Petersfield, he had to stop the car and pull into a lay-by.

The headache was blinding him, quite literally. Time went astray. He drifted. When he awoke, it was better enough to continue. Vera was barely able to control her distress when he got back to the bungalow. Slowly, he unravelled the story for her. It was not the fact that their business was gutted, nor the under-insurance, nor even the uncertainty about reopening ever again that haunted her. It was that someone who lived with headaches every day had had to stop and sleep which worried her as they lay in bed that night.

Together, we got the business going again, by erecting two corrugated iron garages behind the factory building, putting a power press in one and a welding plant in the other. There was a tarpaulin over the shell of the workshop and, gradually, it became possible to get machinery going again as we cleared the debris from the benches and tools. Everywhere my Dad went, I went too. We usually lunched at the Prince Albert, until one day when he slumped onto the steering wheel of the Humber.

'*I feel terrible,*' he said. He looked awful and didn't eat or drink anything. The next day, he was in bed and, shortly afterwards, he was in hospital. Crisis succeeded crisis as the weeks passed. My favourite time for visiting was Saturday afternoon, when there would be just the two of us. I would report on the state of the business and we'd talk about everything and anything. Sometimes he was quite ill, other times better, but he gradually took less interest in what I told him about his burnt-out hopes in Station Road.

Eventually, Christmas came and, at last, Tony was home. Vera picked him up from the hospital and he entered the house to tumultuous applause, as usual. As well as seasonal decorations, there was 'Welcome Home' bunting. Conveniently, the Sister of the ward he'd been in, lived in our road. Quite discreetly, she called to see him periodically. All through Christmas, Tony told stories of Ireland and his younger days. He played sentimental songs on his new stereo gramophone and sat for hours with Vera. It was wonderful to have him home. On the day after Boxing Day, I went to see a blues show, in Croydon. That evening, he was taken back into hospital.

'There's a song we sing at church, which is bluesy, bordering on boogie-woogie,' I said, as we marched through a pine forest and on towards Powerscourt Waterfall. I had been humming *Praise Him on the Trumpet* for so long that, in my exhaustion, I was singing a wide variety of words. As the falls approached, I said I doubted my ability to continue over such rugged terrain. Surely, if these falls are well known, there will be a road to them. We could follow it to civilisation. I was wrong. The tourist part of this waterfall was much further down-stream. We stopped and drank the clear mountain water, laced with a little of the contents of the whiskey flask. I felt better immediately. We both tried some more. We had no food, since our cheese sandwich was eaten, so we set out again. It was about 1.30 pm.

'Are you alright, mate,' Roger asked again.

'I feel really weird ... shouldn't have had that drink.' By now, I'd given up pretending. I didn't realise at the time how desperate Roger felt about the predicament he'd led me into; after all, we needn't have come at all.

'If I don't lie down, I'm going to fall down.' Through the haze, sweat, shivers and sneezes, I can just remember saying it. Before I went into a misty reverie, I remember wondering how I'd tell everyone that I'd had to give up on the second day.

I looked up as my mother walked into the room, with her brother-in-law, John, holding her arm. He spoke gently to her,

'Sit down, Vera, I'll get you a cup of tea.' She just stood there and spoke quite clearly to me,

'He died at twenty past eight.' It was New Year's Eve.

I looked up and there was my old friend, looking worried and offering to carry my rucksack as well as his own. I had found a new definition of friendship.

'Rog'

'Yes, mate?'

'I think I'm going to be all right.'

Ex Libris Press publishes a range of books on the history and topography of the West Country; also a number of walking guides and volumes of country writing.

For a current catalogue of titles please contact EX LIBRIS PRESS at 1 The Shambles, Bradford-on-Avon, Wiltshire, BA15 1JS. Tel (02216) 3595.